16 HOURS IN HEAVEN

BILL HEMBREE

WestBow
PRESS®
A DIVISION OF THOMAS NELSON
& ZONDERVAN

WestBow Press books may be ordered through booksellers or by contacting:

WestBow Press
A Division of Thomas Nelson & Zondervan
1663 Liberty Drive
Bloomington, IN 47403
www.westbowpress.com
844-714-3454

ISBN: 978-1-6642-7948-3 (sc)
ISBN: 978-1-6642-7949-0 (e)

Library of Congress Control Number: 2022918084

Print information available on the last page.

WestBow Press rev. date: 10/14/2022

I would like to dedicate this book to my wife Beth and my three sons: Will, Thomas, and Miles. My greatest accomplishments in life are marrying Beth and being a father to Will, Thomas, and Miles. Life is measured in many ways. The joy of a relationship that is filled with love carries the highest measure for me.

Beth is my soul mate, wife, best friend, lover, and mother of my children. She is also the love of my life, my partner, and my mate for life.

You may not believe in love at first sight, but it can happen and it happened to me. I was in the lunchroom at Douglas County High School when I saw Beth the first time. I asked my friend John McLarty, "Who is that girl? She is so beautiful!" John said, "Her name is Beth Camp, and she is taken!" I was disappointed that she had a boyfriend. I would see her occasionally in the high school hallway and she was always with the other guy. The year passed by and I was still all alone with nothing but an image of this pretty girl in my mind. I was nearing the end of my senior year in high school.

It was springtime in Georgia and that also means tornado season. During the month of April, our high school had a mandatory tornado drill to prepare the students for severe weather. An alarm sounded and the principal announced that everyone should leave their classroom and sit in the hallway. The hallway was the safest place in school away from glass windows and open doors.

I was in my senior psychology class at the time and suddenly realized this would be my last tornado drill. As we sat in the hall with our backs against the wall, I had a feeling someone was watching me. Someone had their eyes on me. Someone wanted me to look their way. As I turned my head to the right and glanced down the hall, I saw her. I was a little embarrassed and quickly turned the other way. Was she looking at me or someone else? I looked again and she gave me a smile and a wink. I smiled back and with silent lips asked, "Are you looking at me?" She smiled again, and with silent lips, she said yes. I was so excited that I turned the other way. I didn't know what to say. I didn't know what to do.

Suddenly, the alarm sounded and the principal ordered everyone to return to class. As I stood up, I got the courage to walk down and meet her. I said, "My name is Bill." She said, "My name is Beth." The teacher was calling, so I asked Beth if I could meet her after class. She said yes. So I walked her to class that day and every day during our high school days together. Beth became my high school sweetheart, and later she became my wife.

God blessed Beth and me with three incredible sons. They are an amazing gift from God. Fatherhood has been the most enjoyable job I have ever had. The job of being a dad never ends. It is highlighted with the greatest reward of love and respect. Helping a baby grow to a little boy. Helping a little boy grow to a teenager. Helping a teenager grow to become a young man. Helping a young man grow to become a respectable adult.

These steps are wonderful achievements. Building character and watching the boys grow to display my teachings give me overwhelming pride. I taught them to lead by example and make wise decisions. They each have unique gifts and talents. They are disciplined and motivated to find success in life. I once heard that life has no roadmap, so the best way to travel is listening to the advice of your dad.

I am rewarded when they asked me for advice and seek my help. I have made a lifetime of mistakes and hope they are not repeated. It is so pleasing to watch my sons grow and experience the goodness of life.

I want to thank my wife and sons for helping me and inspiring me to become a better husband and dad. I want to thank them for loving me unconditionally.

I dedicate this book to my four greatest accomplishments in life: Beth, Will, Thomas, and Miles.

The Hembree Family.

In the beginning God created the heavens and the earth.
The earth was without form and void, and darkness was over the face of the
deep. And the Spirit of God was hovering over the face of the waters.
And God said, "Let there be light," and there was light..
And God saw that the light was good. And God separated the light from the darkness.
God called the light Day, and the darkness he called Night. And
there was evening and there was morning, the first day.
And God said, "Let there be an expanse in the midst of the
waters, and let it separate the waters from the waters."
And God made the expanse and separated the waters that were under the
expanse from the waters that were above the expanse. And it was so.
And God called the expanse Heaven. And there was evening
and there was morning, the second day.
And God said, "Let the waters under the heavens be gathered together
into one place, and let the dry land appear." And it was so.
God called the dry land Earth, and the waters that were gathered
together he called Seas. And God saw that it was good.
And God said, "Let the earth sprout vegetation, plants yielding seed, and fruit trees bearing
fruit in which is their seed, each according to its kind, on the earth." And it was so.
The earth brought forth vegetation, plants yielding seed according to their own kinds, and trees
bearing fruit in which is their seed, each according to its kind. And God saw that it was good.
And there was evening and there was morning, the third day.
And God said, "Let there be lights in the expanse of the heavens to separate the day
from the night. And let them be for signs, and for seasons, and for days, and years.
and let them be lights in the expanse of the heavens to give light upon the earth." And it was so.
And God made two great lights—the greater light to rule the day
and the lesser light to rule the night—and the stars.
And God set them in the expanse of the heavens to give light on the earth,

to rule over the day and over the night, and to separate the light
from the darkness. And God saw that it was good.
And there was evening and there was morning, the fourth day.
And God said, "Let the waters swarm with swarms of living creatures, and
let birds fly above the earth across the expanse of the heavens."
So God created the great sea creatures and every living creature that moves,
with which the waters swarm, according to their kinds, and their kind, and
every winged bird according to its kind. And God saw that it was good.
And God blessed them, saying, "Be fruitful and multiply, and fill the
waters in the seas, and let birds multiply on the earth."
And there was evening and there was morning, the fifth day.
And God said, "Let the earth bring forth the living creatures according to their kinds—
livestock and creeping things and beast of the earth according to their kinds." And it was so.
And God made the beasts of the earth according to their kinds and the
livestock according to their kinds, and everything that creeps on the
ground according to its kind. And God saw that it was good.
Then God said, "Let us make man in our image, after our likeness. And let them have
domain over the fish of the sea and over the birds of the heavens and over the livestock
and over all the earth, and over every creeping thing that creeps on the earth."
So God created man in his own image, in the image of God
created he him; male and female created he them.
And God blessed them. And God said to them, "Be fruitful and multiply and fill
the earth and subdue it, and have dominion over the fish of the sea and over the
birds of the heavens and over every living thing that moves on the earth."
And God said, "Behold, I have given you every plant yielding seed that is on the face
of all the earth, and every tree with seed in its fruit. You shall have them for food.
And to every beast of the earth and to every bird of the heavens and to
everything that creeps on the earth, everything that has the breath of
life, I have given every green plant for food." And it was so.
And God saw everything that he had made, and behold, it was very good.
And there was evening and there was morning, the sixth day.
—Genesis 1:1–31 (English Standard Version)

Thus, the heavens and the earth were finished, and all the host of them.
And on the seventh day God finished his work that he had done, and he
rested on the seventh day from all his work that he had done.
—Genesis 2:1–2 (ESV)

The creation of all things was from God. Man and woman were created in the image of God. Life is a gift from God. Children are a gift from God; they are a reward from Him. Jesus said, "Let the little children come to me, and do not hinder them, for the kingdom of heaven belongs to such as these."
—Matthew 19:14 (New International Version)

I was born at 2:45 a.m. on Tuesday, March 8, 1966. The hospital was in a small town called Villa Rica, Georgia. My mother was Monta Raye Buchanan Hembree, and my father was Aubrey Herman Hembree. I was their fifth child, and they named me William Aubrey Hembree. My sisters are Arubra Gardner and Vista Richardson. My brothers are Phil Hembree and Johnny Hembree. Remarkably, all five children were born at Villa Rica Hospital and delivered by Dr. John Powell.

This is the beginning of my story and my journey through life.

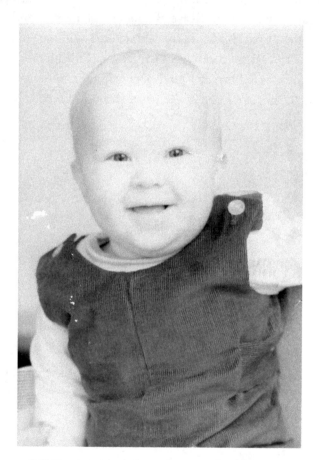

Bill Hembree as a baby at three months old in 1966.

HONOR YOUR FATHER AND MOTHER

Blessed are the poor in spirit, for theirs is the Kingdom of Heaven.
—Matthew 5:3 (NIV)

When you are poor as a child, it often goes unnoticed if you live with a family that is rich in love. My family was rich in love and poor in spirit. The seven members of my family lived in a two-bedroom and one-bathroom home. I never noticed how small our house was or the limited food that we had, but I do know that I was happy. Our tiny house was filled with love, joy, warmth, and happiness. These wonderful emotions were instilled in us by our parents.

Monta Raye and Herman Hembree were exceptional parents. The foundation of who they were and how they acted was based on their Christian faith and hard work. Monta Raye had the most difficult and rewarding job in the world as a mother of five children. She was a homemaker and spent her days taking care of the children. Herman was a very hardworking blue-collar man. He had the very difficult job of finding water and drilling water wells for homes and businesses around Georgia. This hard labor job required strength and knowledge. He was involved in a constant search as he bore holes deep into the earth to find life-giving and thirst-quenching water. The cold days of winter and the hot days of summer never stopped this hardworking man from finding water.

In the Bible, the word *water* is used as a symbol for salvation and eternal life. God offers us salvation and eternal life in the kingdom of heaven through faith in his son Jesus Christ. Water is very important in our Christian walk of faith. God mentions the word *water* 722 times in the Bible. *Water* is used more than *faith, hope, prayer,* and *worship.* John 7:37–38 (NKJV) says, "On the last day, that great day of the feast, Jesus stood up and cried out, 'If anyone thirst, let him come to me and drink. He who believes in me, as the Scripture has said, out of his heart will flow rivers of living water.'"

The Bible also tells us the story of the Samaritan woman who met Jesus by the well.

> Jesus said, "If you knew the gift of God, and who it is that is saying to you, 'Give me a drink,' you would have asked him, and he would have given you living water."

The woman said to him, "Sir, you have nothing to draw water with, and the well is deep. Where do you get that living water? Are you greater than our father Jacob? He gave us the well and drank from it himself, as did his sons and his livestock." Jesus said to her, "Everyone who drinks of this water will be thirsty again, but whoever drinks of the water that I will give him will never be thirsty again. The water that I will give him will become in him a spring of water welling up to eternal life." The woman said to him, "Sir, give me this water, so that I will not be thirsty or have to come here to draw water." (John 4:10–15 ESV)

John 3:5 (NIV) Jesus also said, "Very truly I tell you, no one can enter the kingdom of God unless they are born of water and the Spirit." In water baptism, you are being baptized in the name of Jesus, with the purpose of cleansing your body and washing away your old sinful ways and a new life of forgiveness in the name of our Savior, Jesus Christ.

I have three strong and lasting memories of my father. The first was a simple act that filled my heart with joy and excitement. Going to work with my dad. It was just the two of us and we were up early on a Monday morning to begin our adventure. We loaded up in his blue Chevrolet truck and started the drive to Atlanta. I sat right next to my dad in the front seat. Car seats did not exist so I snuggled close to him and he made me cocaptain of driving the truck. My dad checked in at the company office on Monday so he could get his weekly work schedule. He was so proud of me as he held my hand and introduced me to his boss and the ladies he worked with at the office. The office had just installed a new water fountain and my dad lifted me up to take a drink from this new and amazing water machine. I was so excited and happy to spend the day with my dad.

My father traveled during the week drilling water wells across the state of Georgia. This time away from home made him lonely, and he missed the presence of his family. The weekend was family time, and nothing would change that. The family vacation was a requirement so we could all share in fun times and adventures. One great memory was a day trip to Callaway Gardens in the springtime. He planned the trip with our church family so we could all enjoy the beautiful azaleas and blooming spring flowers. Another great adventure full of memories was a camper trip from Georgia to Key West, Florida. One of the many stops was Silver Springs, Florida. A glass-bottom boat carried us around the crystal-clear springs that were absolutely beautiful. I saw the ocean for the first time in my life as we stopped at Miami Beach for a day of fun in the sun and swimming in the surf. After we crossed a seven-mile bridge over the ocean, we reached the southern tip of the United States: the town of Key West.

We never know how much time we have on earth, and my dad believed we should enjoy every precious day and live fully. My dad's life was based on faith, family, and hard work. It may seem like a simple life, but it was a good life for the family he loved. It is hard to understand why tragic events happen in life. Happiness turns to sadness for reasons we cannot comprehend. We must always maintain our faith in God and accept His plan as we travel through life.

It was a September day in 1969 and my dad was on a jobsite drilling a water well. He died from a heart attack. He was just forty-five years old, and I was just a little boy who would grow up without my dad.

Aubrey Herman Hembree, Bill's father.

Growing up without a father was very lonely, but God introduced many people who were influential in my life. Amazing events in my life allowed me to visit the White House in Washington, DC, three times. I met three presidents who were very influential in my life. President Jimmy Carter, President Ronald Reagan, and President George H. W. Bush gave me the honor of speaking with them and sharing ideas about the greatness of our country. Although these men were outstanding and very interesting to meet, it was a group of women who are most influential in my life: my mother, Monta Raye Hembree, my wife, Elizabeth Hembree, my grandmother Martha Jones, and my schoolteacher Sandy Wilson.

Let me begin by telling you the story of my wonderful mother. Monta Raye Buchanan Hembree was born on a cold winter morning in December 1933. Martha Anne Buchanan delivered her at their home in Franklin, North Carolina. In those days, hospitals were only in big cities so Monta Raye was delivered by a midwife at home. They say it was a rough winter for baby Monta Raye. She had the measles with a fever and cough. It affected her eyes, and later when she entered school, she wore glasses because of the damage. The Buchanan family farm was located just outside Franklin in a community called Saunders town. My mother's grandfather and the head of the Buchanan clan was Mr. Benjamin Evans Buchanan. Her grandmother was Isabel Buena Vista Thompson Buchanan. This was all during the Great Depression and times were hard for all people, especially those living in the remote mountains. Martha Anne was a wonderful mother and a strong provider for little Monta Raye. She was called away to find work and left Monta Raye in the loving hands of her grandparents. She was a sweet, little angel for Grandpa and Grandma to care for. They provided a safe and loving home until she was five years old. She had memories of how thoughtful her grandparents were. One year she got overalls and long, brown knee socks for her birthday and patent leather shoes for Christmas. Grandpa had a special love for Monta Raye, and it was he who would comfort her when she was sad. These were tough times during the depression and the government would ration food. Grandpa would make a special order for grapes because grapes were her favorite fruit.

Grandpa had sugar diabetes and died when Mother was six. Although this was a sad day to lose such a loving grandpa, it opened the door of happiness for her. Her mother, Martha Anne, returned to bring Monta Raye to her home. This was in a small community called Otto, North Carolina. This was a very happy time to be reunited with her mother and experiencing the birth of her only brother, Dale. A few years later, a very special delivery arrived. Her baby sister, Andrea, was born. She pretended Andrea was her own little baby and treated her like a princess baby doll. Her family was whole again.

This was a happy time for my mother. She made a lot of girlfriends at school. Every day she led the way as they walked together on their way to school. The family attended a country church, and Mother loved Sunday school. Grandma came to visit one Sunday morning before church. Mother was taking a bath and Grandma was scrubbing her clean for Sunday school. Grandma said she was trying to wash Monta Raye's freckles away. Monta Raye said, "You can stop. I already tried it, and it doesn't work."

After World War II ended, Martha Anne left the mountains of North Carolina and moved to the great state of Georgia. Martha found a steady paying job at a sewing factory in Atlanta. Monta Raye, Dale, and Andrea were with her and they lived in West Fulton County. They all enrolled in school, and Monta Raye attended West Fulton High School. Martha then connected with her brother Wade Buchanan, and they moved to the Fairplay community in South Douglas County. Monta Raye transferred to Douglas County High School.

She was a good basketball player and got the nickname Speedy for her fast moves on the court. Her high school yearbook said, "Monta Raye Speedy Buchanan." She graduated in 1952.

In the early 1950s, a hot spot for teenagers was the swimming pools at Johnson Lake. Our uncle Paul and aunt Lois owned and operated these swimming pools on Post Road in Winston, Georgia. In the summer of 1952, it was said that our father, Herman Hembree, was a handsome lifeguard. Well, there was a new girl in town, and her name was Monta Raye. She didn't think he would notice her on that summer day, but Herman Hembree did see that pretty blonde girl, and it was love at first sight. They dated through the summer and fall of 1952 and became two lovebirds. They spent all their time together visiting family and friends. They did some fun and silly things that included raccoon hunting. Yes, Monta Raye went raccoon hunting during the night. The raccoon hunting group included Monta Raye, Herman, mother's brother, Dale, and their lifelong friends Ed and Sarah Norton. I know my mother, and she loved Herman, so my guess is nighttime raccoon hunting in South Douglas County was a good excuse for romantic parking.

Well, the romance blossomed and turned into a proposal. On April 30, 1953, Aubrey Herman Hembree asked Monta Raye Buchanan to marry him, and she said yes. The two lovebirds wasted no time. They went to the justice of the peace and were married at the Middle Courthouse on Post Road in Winston. As a wedding present, Herman drove Monta Raye, still wearing her wedding dress, all the way to Franklin, North Carolina, in his 1950 Chevrolet sedan. They surprised her aging grandma Isabel Buena Vista Buchanan with this exciting news. They took pictures and celebrated with family and friends.

When the newlyweds returned to Douglas County, they rented an old home from my uncle Paul and aunt Lois. One morning Monta Raye woke up and said, "Herman, I can see chickens under the floor of our bedroom. We need to move." Well, Herman wasted no time and found Monta Raye her dream home. He bought the two-bedroom and one-bath home from Buford Keaton. Their new address was 5746 Post Road, Winston, Georgia, 30187. This palace on Hembree Hill would be Monta Raye's home for the next sixty-three years! The rest of her life.

I am happy to say that my mother started a career with an insurance company in Atlanta. She carpooled with her sister-in-law, Wilma Strickland, and Mr. Parker along Highway 78 to Atlanta from Monday through Friday. Well, Monta Raye soon decided that being a mother and homemaker was a much better job for her. The Hembree family was about to grow.

At just over four pounds, baby number one came into this world and Monta Raye and Herman named her Arubra. When Arubra turned one, Monta Raye told Herman, "We need a family picture." They hired a professional photographer and were getting dressed for the picture. Monta Raye said, "You know, Herman, my favorite color is pink." Well, Herman, who was a blue-collar, outdoors, strong man with a nickname of Bull, came out dressed in a pink shirt. The first Hembree picture of Herman, Monta Raye, and little Arubra was absolutely beautiful.

Monta Raye would do anything to help her children. Arubra's elementary school class held a fundraiser. Our family was not rich, but Mother was determined to help Arubra. She sold chances for people to win a Bird of Paradise Avon gift set. She sold so many tickets that Arubra won the class fundraiser.

Then came baby number two, and Herman said, "It's a boy!" Monta Raye got to name her baby boy. She loved a Hollywood movie actor from the 1940s and 1950s. His name was John Cameron Swayze. So they welcomed into the world Phil Cameron Hembree. Phil played the most remarkable role in our mother's life. When our dad died, Phil was only twelve years old. One of our uncles told Phil, "You are the man of the household now." Those words changed him forever, and he led the Hembree household flawlessly.

The Hembree family continue to grow with baby number three. Again, Herman said, "It's a boy!" And this time, he got to name his son. Herman's dad was Johnny Hembree and his favorite uncle was Walter. So the baby boy was named Johnny Walter Hembree. Johnny and our mother share the same birthday in December. Monta Raye thought her baby Johnny had the prettiest face. Gerber baby food was as popular in the 1950s as it is today. Gerber had a national contest to find the prettiest baby in America. Well, Monta Raye felt she had a winner and entered Johnny in the national contest.

Mother was a protector of her children. When Arubra started the first grade, she loaded her up on the school bus. Mother couldn't let go of Arubra, so she quickly grabbed Phil and baby Johnny. She loaded them up in the blue Chevy Impala. She followed the school bus all the way to Winston Elementary School to make sure Arubra was safe. Arubra played her part by sitting in the backseat of the bus and waving to Mother, Phil, and Johnny all the way down the road.

Monta Raye and Herman welcomed baby number four, and she was a precious little girl. They joined to select the perfect name. Herman said, "We should name her after you," and Monta Raye picked her sweet grandma, Isabell Buena Vista Buchanan. So they gave her the name Monta Vista Hembree. As the baby daughter with a caring nature, Vista shared a special bond with Mother during the final years of her life. She bathed her, rolled her hair, painted her nails, rubbed lotion on her feet, and treated our mother in a very special way.

Mother took a job at Winston Elementary School so she could drive Vista to school and be with her all day. She got her summers off work and we enjoyed amazing vacations. Monta Raye would plan them. Two of our favorite trips were Savannah and Tybee Island in Georgia and the other was Chattanooga and Lookout Mountain in Tennessee. We also made many trips to the mountains of North Carolina. Cherokee, North Carolina, was also fun, and we often had our picture made with local Indians.

Mother loved to read and write letters and encouraged her children to do the same. She bought many books and magazines for her children in hopes to capture her passion.

I was baby number five in the Hembree family, and my mother named me after my father and her uncle: William Roosevelt Buchanan and my dad, Aubrey Herman Hembree. I am William Aubrey Hembree Sr. My mother called me Baby Bill.

All five of Monta Raye and Herman's children were born at Villa Rica Hospital. They were all delivered by Dr. John Powell, and each rode home from the hospital in an ambulance. It was truly remarkable that after delivering five babies in the same hospital many years before, her last breath on earth and death of her body was at Villa Rica hospital.

One of Mother's greatest legacies is her grandchildren, great-grandchildren, and great-great-grandchildren. When her grandchildren were babies, her greatest pleasure was gathering them all up and taking a Sunday afternoon nap. She babysat them and never missed a birthday or celebration. They called her Granny Raye and Mae Mae.

On Tuesday, September 30, 1969, tragedy struck. Monta Raye's beloved husband, Aubrey Herman Hembree, died. Herman drilled water wells for the Atlanta company Virginia Supply and Wells. Mother once told me when Daddy left for the jobsite on Monday morning that he didn't feel good. She recommended that he go to his doctor. His job was in Monroe, Georgia, that week, and he didn't have time to see a doctor. Sometime around three o'clock in the afternoon on that Tuesday, Daddy must have had chest pains. He was working alone so he sat under a large oak tree to rest. He suffered a massive heart attack and died. At five o'clock, Herman was to check in at a general store in Monroe. When he didn't show up, the store owner went to the jobsite. He found our dad in the field under the big oak tree. Mr. Martin, the owner of Virginia Supply and Wells, called Monta Raye that evening to tell her that Herman had passed away.

Mother once told me that she was absolutely heartbroken. The love of her life was gone. She also told me her emotions hardened and she became very angry. How could this happen? She was a homemaker with five children. This is when her faith in God took over to start healing her broken heart.

Herman was a strong Christian man, and when Mother moved to Douglas County, he encouraged her to join his church, the Methodist Church. So in 1954, Monta Raye joined Herman and became a member of the Flint Hill Methodist Church. Today, that church is called New Covenant United Methodist. It was the church members and her family who helped Mother and directed her on what to do in continuing her life without her beloved husband.

Monta Raye Hembree, Bill's mother.

It was exactly fifty years after Herman's death that Monta Raye died and left this earth to touch the face of God. Monta Raye and Herman are buried next to one another at the old Flint Hill Church Cemetery. Their earthly bodies and love are side by side once again.

Monta Raye was a thirty-five-year-old widow with five children. Herman was a wise man and bought a $5,000 life insurance policy. Mother knew her children were growing and they all shared one bedroom in her house. She made a great decision and used the life insurance to build two more bedrooms and a new bathroom onto her home. This was her home, and it was paid for. This home was a permanent foundation for her young family filled with memories and love.

Growing up during the Great Depression, Mother was surrounded by family who had extraordinary work ethics. She had a saying that if you work, you will survive. She had a part-time job selling Avon beauty supplies. Now that job became full time. She was selling Avon door to door with her children joining her. The old blue Chevrolet Impala car was not reliable, and taking her kids to work with her was not working. Mother always wanted to be close to her kids, and she loved to cook. She needed another job to meet their needs. Vista, Johnny, Phil, and Arubra were students at Winston Elementary School, so she applied for a cooking job in the school cafeteria. She got hired, and the job was perfect. She worked at the school cafeteria for eighteen years. Cafeteria work was hard, but she enjoyed her daily role of cooking, passing out desserts, and making sure the children picked up their milk. Her favorite dessert to make was those delicious peanut butter bars. The most important part of this job was being close to her children.

The cafeteria job was great, but she needed more money to support her children. There was a café in Winston that was a hot spot and popular with all the locals. In fact, this restaurant was one of the best in Georgia. It was called Rock Inn Café. Two wonderful people, Burnell and Betty Redding, owned the restaurant and hired Monta Raye as a waitress. Mother was a waitress every Friday and Saturday night. Monta Raye liked people so she was an excellent waitress. The café closed at 9 p.m. so Mother was always home to kiss her children good night. A great waitress makes good tips. She usually made $60 each night. Most of her tips were paid in quarters, so I got to help her roll those quarters before bed so she could deposit them into her bank on Monday.

Mother worked at the Rock Inn Café for eighteen years. She never complained and worked hard at both jobs six days a week for eighteen years. Mother's incredible work ethic provided enough money to buy food and clothing her children needed. Mother was in her fifties now and realized she needed some kind of retirement income. Every week she shopped at the Winn-Dixie grocery store. The store manager had heard she was a great cook and knew she had a great personality. He offered her a job with benefits working in the bakery.

She took the job and left the other two jobs. So every morning she was up at 4 a.m. to work at 5 a.m., so she could bake the morning doughnuts. Making bear claws was her favorite pastry. She usually had Taco Bell for lunch and saved time for a short fifteen-minute nap in her car in the parking lot. Getting up at 4 a.m. was hard on her body so she needed to rest. She gave a free cookie to children who passed the bakery just like she gave dessert to the kids at Winston Elementary School.

When Mother retired, I asked her what her favorite job was: Avon, Winston Elementary School, Rock Inn Café, or Winn-Dixie. She said that was an easy question. It was Rock Inn Café. She loved waiting on friends, talking to people, and meeting new friends. She said all the people at Rock Inn Café were like her family.

Monta Raye never met a stranger. She had no fear and loved to travel. She would go on trips, cruises, and church trips whenever one was available. She often traveled alone during her retirement years because she knew she would meet others and enjoy their company. Mother met some rich and famous people in her life.

My wife, Beth, and I won a business trip to California and invited Mother to come along. We took Mother to see the beautiful coastal California town called Monterey. After all, they shared the same name. I was trying to find a parking space in downtown Monterey, when my mother, Monta Raye said, "Stop the car. I see him!" She and Beth jumped out of the moving car. When I got the car stopped, I too saw him. It was the movie star and Academy award winner Kevin Costner. He was with his bodyguards going to an event. Even with two wild ladies running after him, he was a true gentleman. Mother hugged him, kissed him, and got a picture made with the one and only Kevin Costner. After that day, if you asked her what her favorite movie was, there was no question, it was *Dances with Wolves* starring Kevin Costner of course.

In 1985, Mother traveled with me to the National DECA Conference in San Francisco, California. The star entertainment at the convention was music singer Donny Osmond. Mother got the privilege of meeting Donny, sitting next to him before he performed, and escorting him onto the stage. Onstage in front of 15,000 people, she said, "Donny, you know purple is one of my favorite colors? Are you wearing purple socks tonight?" Donny said, "Yes, Mrs. Hembree, I am wearing purple socks!" Mother said, "I am a little bit country!" Donny said, "I'm a little bit rock 'n' roll!"

Everyone loves a Chick-fil-A sandwich and the company's Christian values. The owner and founder, Truett Cathy, became a billionaire. He was a very godly man and a true American success story. I met Mr. Cathy when I was the high school DECA president. Mother joined me when Mr.

Cathy gave us a private tour of his company headquarters in Atlanta. Mr. Cathy was humbled when my mother told him her life story. They were friends. As the years went by and I saw Truett Cathy, the first thing he always asked was "How's your mother doing?"

Mother loved music. Elvis was her favorite singer, and in 1978 we took a family trip to Memphis, Tennessee, to visit his home called Graceland. Music and the lyrics of songs allowed her to escape the loneliness, sadness, and hardships of life. During the evening after work, she would play the love ballad records by artist like Marty Robbins, Freddie Fender, and of course Elvis.

There are not enough words to describe the beautiful person that Monta Raye Hembree was on this earth. I realized you don't have to be a soldier to be a fighter and survivor. You just have to be a person like my mother. I cannot imagine the grief and pain she felt when our father died. I only know that she never wavered. Putting her grief and pain away and focusing on raising her five children was what she lived for each day. She was one of the most selfless, loving ladies I have ever known. She focused on her family, her church, her job, and her community.

She placed the foundation of our family on the actions of faith and love. She never had to tell us to read our Bibles, to pray, or to have faith because she showed us this in her daily actions. Her Bible was used and her faith was challenged, but she never gave up or wore down to life's struggles. There is a story in the Bible of a widow's mite. She gave us an example of tithing at church. With her folded dollar bills placed in the offering plate, she taught us that it wasn't in the amount that you gave but in the fact of giving to God. She knew with faithful obedience that God would meet all our needs.

I never heard her gossip or put other people down with judgment. She always said that the only person we can change in this world is ourselves. God gave her many gifts. She was a prolific letter writer, phone caller, and visitor to friends and those in need.

In my mother's home, her house on the hill, her living room was her comfort and safe place. She always lay on her sofa. Above her head was a collection of angels. Next to that was a picture of Jesus and the Last Supper. The other walls were covered with pictures of her children and grandchildren that home was heaven on earth for our mother. God blessed us for eighty-five years with the presence of a remarkable lady called Monta Raye.

Bill, Johnny, Monta Raye, Phil, Vista and Arubra Hembree on Christmas Day.

BROTHERS AND SISTERS

A strong family with faith in God is the foundation that helped me grow into adulthood. Children are a gift from God, and having five kids is a true blessing. The five of us have a unique bond that comes from the example set by our parents. Our father's death galvanized our relationship, and our mother guided us to love one another, help one another, and stay close together to overcome life's challenges.

My sister Arubra is a wonderful person. She has a heart that is filled with love and compassion for others. God has given her a special gift of encouragement and connecting with people. She has never met a stranger and has the largest circle of friends I have ever known. She is a true friend and a best friend to all those she loves. She never misses a birthday or special event and encourages everyone to share special time together. Her spirit is filled with kindness and generosity. Cards, flowers, and personal visits from her lift the spirits of those she encounters. Her energy level cannot be matched as she fills the world with good deeds. Her kind words and happy smile make our world a better place. Her Christian faith is so powerful and noticeable with all the goodness she brings to life. Her empathy helps her understand the struggles people face daily in life. She is sincere, people trust her with their feelings, and she supports them to help make things better. She is friendly, nice, and easy to get along with. She's enthusiastic, and her positive attitude is contagious. Arubra is a remarkable woman.

My brother Phil is a great man. God has given him the gift of wisdom and knowledge. The world we live in confronts us with changing ideas that are sometimes against biblical principles. Phil's Christian faith is a solid foundation in the principles he holds that are true and unwavering. Phil believes the Bible is God's Word and should never be manipulated or changed to conform to society. He is straightforward with his message and a true conservative. He is honest and takes responsibility for his actions. He has integrity and self-control and makes good decisions to help others. He is the most reliable person I know, and you can always count on him for help. He is loyal to his family and friends. He has the courage to stand up for what he believes in and the courage to defend the truth. He is a compassionate caregiver and never complains about his responsibilities. He has a problem-solving mind that is engineered to fix a broken world. His work ethic is remarkable, and he will never give you an excuse to avoid work. Phil is truly a good and faithful servant to our Lord Jesus Christ.

My brother Johnny is a great man. God has given him a creative mind. His creativity allows him to think about ways to find solutions with unconventional methods. He is a problem-solver and eager to get the job done. He is a craftsman and very skilled at doing his work. If you have something broken, he can fix it. He is a great one-on-one communicator and very knowledgeable with his discussions. He likes to talk with you and not at you. Just friendly conversations that develop into strong bonds for the people he calls friends. He enjoys time with his family and friends. He is loyal to those he loves and a powerful defender for everyone he cares about. He has a likable personality and finds it easy to make new friends. He has a warm heart and a kind spirit. He has a passion for helping others who struggle in life. He is an overcomer and has met life's challenges with renewed strength. Johnny has been saved by the grace of God. He finds freedom in his faith and salvation from his Savior Jesus Christ.

My sister Vista is a wonderful person. God has given Vista a caring heart and a passion to help others. She will help you and take care of you. She will love you and encourage you. She will hold you and lift you up. She will calm you with her voice. She will guide you with peaceful solutions. She is a faithful friend and will never abandon you. She has unconditional love for her family and friends. She will support you and defend you with every fiber of her being. Her loyalty is steadfast. She is very intelligent and uses her mind to find ways to help others. She has compassion and feels sympathy for the suffering and misfortune of others. Her generosity is a wonderful gift for everyone she encounters. She has a kind spirit and always puts others first. She is a comforter to those in need and nurtures those she loves. Hard work and the satisfaction of a job well done is her trademark. There is no job too little or too much that she can't handle. She is humble and accepts life's challenges with a quiet demeanor. She cherishes the freedom of life, and her free spirit gives her joy and satisfaction. She believes in the natural connection of all God's creations. She sees the earth as God's garden for healing and sustaining life. She is fearless with determination and has an open mind about the world around her. She is adventurous and sees the world as a gift from God. Her faith is the foundation that carries her through life. The Holy Spirit and the spirit of Jesus Christ shine brightly in her soul. She is saved by grace and a gift to the world.

Phil, Vista, Johnny, Arubra and Bill Hembree

A GRANDMOTHER'S LOVE

God gives us His unconditional love. For God so loved the world that He gave His only begotten Son, that whoever believes in Him should not perish but have everlasting life. God has a different plan for each of us and sometimes we don't understand the circumstances in life that we must deal with daily. My grandfather died before I was born, and my father died when I was a little boy. My life was missing those two incredible figures to help mold me into the person I would grow to become. God filled this void in my life with two amazing women who gave me more love than I could ever imagine: my mother and grandmother.

My grandmother, Martha Anne, was a kind and gentle woman. Living through the Great Depression was a challenge for everyone, and Martha survived that hardship. She experienced love that turned into broken romances. It seems she replaced relationships with survival, and her primary role was taking care of her children.

After my father died and my mother began working two jobs, I needed to be cared for so we turned to my granny. For two years, my mother delivered me to Granny's house. She alone made my stay with her the happiest time in my young life. She introduced me to the concept of having a daily schedule of activities. She had plenty of daily household chores to complete but always made time for me. We took daily walks around her property, and she opened my eyes to the beauty of the world around us.

She loved animals and had dogs and cats as pets outside of her home. Her compassion for these animals was wonderful, and they fulfilled her life with their unconditional love toward her. Every day we fed the dog, fed the cat, and fed the birds. She told me to always take care of God's creations and always feed the animals.

Granny was a terrific cook, and my day was filled with delicious food. She watched me play outside and inside the house and always interacted with me so that I felt safe and happy. Although I was alone with no other children around, she always told me to use my imagination so I could find joy in my activities. Whether I was playing like a cowboy or soldier, climbing a tree, or running with the dog, I never felt alone.

One hour a day was her time, and she introduced me to the TV drama called a soap opera. We watched the show called *Days of our Lives*. It seemed to take her mind away from the routine world around us. Television can sometimes offer the most memorable moments in history. As I sat in her lap one day, she looked at me and told me *Days of Our Lives* would not be on TV. We were going to watch something that would change the world. Man and a spacecraft were going to land on the moon, and we were going to watch it from our living room on earth. It was an unforgettable moment to share with my granny as we watched the Apollo astronauts walk on the moon.

My granny, Martha Anne, gave me unconditional love. She also gave me an example of how to live that became the foundation of who I am today.

Grandmother Martha Anne Buchanan with Bill as a baby.

ELEMENTARY SCHOOL YEARS

After two years of exceptional quality time with my grandmother, I entered the first grade. I was well prepared for this new challenge as my mother had taught me the basics of reading, writing, and arithmetic. The best part of this transition was spending more time with my mother. She worked in the lunchroom so I had the good fortune of riding in her car to school every day. Having her close by in the same building and seeing her at lunchtime made me so happy and gave me a sense of being safe and secure.

I had many great teachers at Winston Elementary School. The most outstanding was Virginia Clay. The first grade is usually so memorable because it is a life-changing time. We did not have kindergarten available in my area, so the first grade was big. Mrs. Clay had just graduated from college and this was her first teaching assignment. Her mind was filled with activities and assignments that we could all enjoy. My mother was a great letter writer and her talent passed on to me. Mrs. Clay designated me as the best handwriter in the first grade. She made a big deal about my penmanship and encouraged the entire class to stop by my desk when we were doing writing exercises. This gave me an enormous amount of pride.

This writing skill got me promoted to a top class the following year. The class was a combination of second and third graders who were star students. Mrs. Clay also introduced me to the idea that through hard work, you can gain rewards. Whenever we answered a question correctly, she would reward us with a tiny marshmallow. I had a sweet tooth and loved marshmallows so I worked extra hard on my homework.

Field day is one of the best days of the year in elementary school. It happens during the warm days of spring when the school year is coming to a close. A day of fun and games is a reward for all the difficult days of classroom work. Some games involve team captains picking their own teams. I was a skinny kid and most of the time was picked last. One of the big events for the day was the wheelbarrow race. Captains picked all of the partners for the race, and guess who was last. Me and a quiet, skinny guy whose name was Eric McCoy. Fifteen teams lined up at the starting point with Eric and me in the last lane. The rule was to have one partner on the ground going down the track and the other partner on the ground coming back. "On your mark, get set, go," said the coach. Although Eric and I were not the best athletes that day, we turned out to be the best team that day.

Our skinny arms and legs worked better and moved faster than all the other teams and we won the race. God put two boys together that day who were in last place and gave us a victory to show the world that teamwork is a winning combination.

Mother always said that idle time can be a bad time. So she signed me up for little league baseball, youth football, Cub Scouts, and chorus. I was not a great athlete and survived one season of football. I did enjoy playing baseball for three seasons. I will never forget my first baseball game and my first opportunity to bat. My coaches were Franklin Richardson and Larry Argo. Coach Richardson put me in the game during the last inning. The score was tied, the bases were loaded, and there were two outs. My coach called me Billy. He said, "Billy, we need a base hit or a walk and we will win the game. You can do it. I believe in you."

I was terrified as I entered the batter's box. How would I do with the pressure of the entire game on my shoulders? The pitcher was much taller and stronger than me. He struck out several of my teammates with his fastball. He drew back and delivered the pitch, and something terrible happened. He lost control of the ball and it hit me in the head. The pitch knocked me out and I was lying on the ground. I don't remember much except the ball heading for my face and then pain over my head.

I woke up a few seconds later with my coach rubbing my head and asking if I was OK. I said, "Yes, sir, I'm OK. I just have a headache." He said, "Billy, you are a hero because we just won the game." By getting hit in the head with a pitch, I automatically went to first base, driving in the winning run.

As a kid, I always wanted to grow up and be a forest ranger. My love for animals, the great outdoors, and fishing made me a great candidate for the Cub Scouts. Mr. Donevill Zachery Sr. was my leader. He was a great leader and always kind and encouraging to me. One of the big Cub Scout events each year was the Pinewood Derby. Each Cub Scout was given a block of wood. It was my responsibility to carve the wood into a race car. It was also necessary to add weight to the car so it would travel faster down the racetrack. I didn't have a dad to help me with this project. But God always filled that empty void.

My neighbor Bobby Kile had a woodworking business. I asked him if he would help me with my Cub Scouts project. He said yes, and we turned that block of wood into a great-looking race car. We had two racing secrets in our wooden car. We placed melted lead in the front of my car with the extra weight carrying it faster down the track. The second secret was placing oil around the wheels so they would spin faster.

When Pinewood Derby day arrived at the Cub Scouts camp, I won every race. I was the Pinewood Derby champion, and we all celebrated the victory together. Mr. Zachery pinned the gold medal on my uniform, and I was so happy and proud.

My entire family loved music. We had an old record player in our living room and the turntable was always rotating with wonderful sounds. My mother loved country music and my brothers and

16 HOURS IN HEAVEN

sisters love rock 'n' roll. In my opinion, the 1970s produced the best bands and the best music of all time. The Carpenters, the Eagles, Paul McCartney and Wings, Queen, ELO, and the Bee Gees had albums my family played all of the time. We watched the *American Bandstand* on TV on Saturdays and listened to Casey Kasem's *Top 40* radio show on Sunday afternoons.

We were very poor with money but rich with sound. We couldn't afford a piano or a guitar so Mother encouraged us to sing. Mrs. Williamson, my fourth-grade music teacher, said I had an excellent voice. She encouraged me to try out for the Atlanta Boy Choir. I was extremely shy and afraid to perform in public so I told her no.

Bill played little league baseball for the Winston cubs.

MISTAKES IN LIFE

We all make mistakes in life and disappoint those who love us. In Romans 7:21–25 (NLT), Paul says, "I have discovered this principle of life—that when I want to do what is right, I inevitably do what is wrong. I love God's law with all my heart. But there is another power within me that is at war with my mind. This power makes me a slave to the sin that is still within me. Oh, what a miserable person I am! Who will free me from this life that is dominated by sin and death? Thank God! The answer is in Jesus Christ our Lord. So you see how it is: In my mind I really want to obey God's law, but because of my sinful nature I am a slave to sin." Jesus has set me free. Life is filled with choices and decision-making. Your mind and your heart are faced daily with the emotional human process of making good decisions or bad decisions. The Holy Spirit inside us is the voice of Jesus, and those who have a strong Christian faith can make the right decisions with confidence. But there is an evil, lower nature inside all of us that pulls us into sinful actions and bad decisions. Who will free us from this evil lower nature and sinful ways? Thank God, it has been done through our Savior Jesus Christ.

Youth can be a very challenging time of life. You may grow up in a loving Christian family that promotes strong Christian values and good character. But a young mind without life experiences can be influenced by the temptations and pressure of the world.

There were two occasions in elementary school that I allowed older friends to pressure me and influence me into doing something that was wrong and illegal. The first disaster involved underage drinking of alcohol. My older friend bought two six-packs of beer and convinced me that getting drunk would be the most amazing feeling I ever had. He then convinced me that drinking a bottle of wine would make the feeling even better. Well, my small elementary school mind and body made the bad decision to do this. I became a drunken fool and eventually passed out. I was so sick when I woke up that I stayed overnight at my so-called friend's house. I never told my mother about this horrible mistake.

The other event that happened in elementary school was smoking cigarettes and watching my older friends smoke marijuana. This happened during the 1970s and seemed acceptable in my eyes for adults so I made the mistake of trying it, too, even though I was a child. I knew this was wrong and I felt so guilty after each event, but that evil, lower nature inside me and the pressure from friends around me said it was OK.

I will never forget the first time I lied. Our family was poor so my mother signed me up for the free lunch program at our elementary school. I didn't know, and my mother didn't know, that I would be interviewed in order to qualify for free lunches. During class, with all my friends around, the teacher called me to his desk to ask me a series of bureaucratic questions. There was no privacy and all of the information was open for everyone to hear. This was one of the most uncomfortable days of my life.

I never told my friends or my teachers that my father had died. No one else in my class had experienced such a tragic event. All of my friends and classmates had a mother and father at home. I didn't want to be different. I wanted to be like everyone else. So this was my secret. In a loud voice, the first question that my teacher asked me was "What job does your father have?" I was in shock and very embarrassed. How would I keep my secret of being different? I lied. Even though I knew it was wrong, I lied anyway. I said in a loud voice for all to hear that my father worked for a well-drilling company. Each question was gut-wrenching because I was openly lying. I lied ten times that day to each question because I couldn't simply say that my father died. It was easier to lie than tell the truth because I didn't want to be different. I wanted a whole family with a mother and father just like my friends had in their homes.

You can't run away from your problems. We face challenges every day and the best approach to deal with them is to solve them with wisdom following Christian principles. Don't delay action. Face every challenge with immediate action and move on with life. When I was a kid, I didn't know how to deal with trouble. The easiest thing for me to do was run away and hide. I felt if I hid long enough, my troubles would go away. I became lazy and depressed. Schoolwork and friendships didn't matter to me, and it was easy to stop trying. I became a poor student and isolated myself to be alone without friends. I missed over thirty days of school one year because I was afraid of that world. I was not smart, I was not popular, I was not an athlete, I thought I looked ugly, and I felt different from everyone else. I couldn't face the daily drama that school offered. Fortunately, I didn't fail the classes because I completed extra assignments. I finally broke out of my depression and realized that you can't run away from your problems and mistakes.

Bill Hembree in the 4th grade.

ALCOHOLISM

I am not an alcoholic, but a member of my family has dealt with this horrible addiction for most of their life. Addictions happen to many people for many reasons. I know that alcohol creates a temporary feeling that is good. It temporarily removes the pain and problems people face daily. It creates a mind-altering numbness in your body that allows some people to escape from reality. Alcohol is a habit-causing drug that is easier to continue using daily without concern for the people around you. Casual and social drinking in our society is so acceptable that I can understand why people can't control this addiction. The craving for a drink can be so overwhelming to an alcoholic that it becomes impossible for them to resist.

Sometimes, the people most affected by alcoholism are the family members and friends who unconditionally love the alcoholic. Decisions affect everyone around you, especially those who love you most. So many terrible things can happen to someone who's drunk and out of control. Their lives are in danger, their marriages and children are in danger, and their financial stability is in danger. Why do people risk so much in order to gain temporary satisfaction? How can alcohol be worth more than your marriage, your children, your home, or your job? I have seen firsthand how all of these wonderful gifts in life can be destroyed by alcoholism. How can you give up so much in life because you can't stop drinking?

I've learned through experience in life that you can't change an alcoholic. The alcoholic is the only one who can make the decision to change their life.

You who are young, be happy while you are young, and let your heart give you joy
in the days of your youth. Follow the ways of your heart and whatever your eyes
see, but know that for all these things God will bring you into judgment.
—Ecclesiastes 11:9 (NIV)

There is a time for everything, and a season for every activity under the heavens:
a time to be born and a time to die, a time to plant and a time to uproot,
a time to kill and a time to heal, a time to tear down and a time to build,
a time to weep and a time to laugh, a time to mourn and a time to dance,
a time to scatter stones and a time to gather them, a time to
embrace and a time to refrain from embracing,
a time to search and the time to give up, a time to keep and a time to throw away,
a time to tear and a time to mend, a time to be silent and a time to speak,
a time to love and a time to hate, a time of war and a time for peace.
—Ecclesiastes 3:1–8 (NIV)

Adolescence is a transition from childhood to becoming an adult. It is often a very difficult period of life as our minds and bodies are overwhelmed with changes. In my opinion, the Bible book of Ecclesiastes best illustrates this transitional time of life. We are young and filled with life, but the seasons of life are approaching as quickly. During this time, it seems that we are forever young and the challenges of the world are faraway.

Throughout the Bible are scriptures that tell us that God gives every person free will. Free will is determined by the choices we make in life. God gives us the freedom or free will to make decisions that can lead to prosperity or destruction. Those years as a teenager usually mark a period of separation from your parents. As a child, you are guided and directed by your parents and they make decisions for you. The period of adolescence opens the door to being an adult and making lifelong decisions that can affect every season of your life.

As I have said before, my love for music started with my mother's love for music. The most meaningful opportunity for me as a teenager was joining my middle school chorus. I didn't have a great voice but sounded OK singing in a group. I was blessed with two remarkable chorus teachers who made an unforgettable difference in my life. Peggy Killian and Sheryl LeClair were excellent teachers and gifted musicians. I was a very shy young man with very little talent. These two amazing teachers pulled me out of a shell of shyness into a world of music.

Every year, Peggy Killian and Sheryl LeClair produced a spring musical for our school. The shows were so popular that tickets sold out for every performance. The events were filled with musical solos, musical group performances, and dancing. These two amazing teachers asked me to sing a solo for the event. The song they selected for me was "Rocky Mountain High" by John Denver. This was the first time in my life that I was ever recognized to perform in public. I was very excited but very nervous, so I practiced, practiced, practiced every day leading up to the performance. During practice my teachers told me I sounded great. This encouragement was what I needed, and it motivated me to do my best.

Once again, on the night of our event, the spring musical was sold out. All the seats were filled and there was standing room only in the school auditorium. My performance was scheduled to take place during the middle of the show. I was so nervous and my heart was racing. I sat on the stool while performing "Rocky Mountain High" so all I had to think about was remembering the lyrics. Peggy Killian and Sheryl LeClair were my backup musicians and my backup singers. Together, the three of us performed flawlessly. When I finished the last lyrics, I was so happy and filled with positive emotions. The audience clapped and roared with approval. The performance was everything I had hoped for and more.

The Bible tells us to sing praises to the Lord. Come to God and sing praises, sing joyfully, sing a new song. One of the most incredible relationships in the Bible is between God and David. God loves music, and David connected with Him through songs. Heaven is filled with music and David sang for the Lord.

Sing to God, sing in praise of his name, extol him who rides on the clouds; rejoice before him, his name is the Lord. A father to the fatherless, a defender of widows, is God in his holy dwelling. (Psalm 68:4–5 NIV)

I will praise you, Lord, among the nations; I will sing of you among the peoples. (Psalm 108:3 NIV)

My lips will shout for joy when I sing praise to you, I whom you have delivered. (Psalm 71:23 NIV)

I will be glad and rejoice in you; I will sing the praises of your name, O Most High. (Psalm 9:2 NIV)

But I will sing of your strength, in the morning I will sing of your love; for you are my fortress, my refuge in times of trouble. (Psalm 59:16 NIV)

You are my hiding place; you will protect me from trouble and surround me with songs of deliverance. (Psalm 32:7 NIV)

But I trust in your unfailing love; my heart rejoices in your salvation. I will sing the Lord's praise, for He has been good to me. (Psalm 13:5–6 NIV)

Because your love is better than life, my lips will glorify you. I will praise you as long as I live, and in your name I will lift up my hands. (Psalm 63:3–4 NIV)

Sing! Sing! Sing! Rejoice in being young.

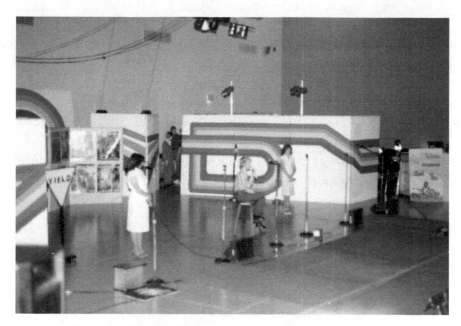

Bill in middle school chorus concert singing Rocky Mountain High.

Bill in 1978 school picture.

YOUNG MEN AND HIGH SCHOOL

Ayoung man needs a mentor or someone who can guide them in the ways of life. Wisdom and common sense are attained through experiences in life. It is so much better to seek advice from those who have encountered the challenges of life. Decisions will come, mistakes will happen, and it is easier to navigate your path with the wisdom and help of others. The Bible gives us wisdom, including for young men.

> Let no one look down on your youthfulness, but rather in speech, conduct, love, faith and purity, show yourself an example of those who believe. (1 Timothy 4:12 New American Standard Bible: 1995

> My son, keep my words and treasure up my commandments with you. (Proverbs 7:1 ESV)

> Now flee from youthful lust and pursue righteousness, faith, love and peace, with those who call on the Lord from a pure heart. (2 Timothy 2:22 NASB95)

> As Jesus was setting out on a journey, a young man ran up and knelt before him and asked him, "Good Teacher, what shall I do to inherit eternal life?" And Jesus said to him, "Why do you call Me good? No one is good except God alone." You know the commandments: Do not murder, Do not commit adultery, Do not steal, Do not bear false witness, Do not defraud, Honor your father and mother." And he said to Him, "Teacher, I have kept all these things from my youth up." Looking at him, Jesus felt a love for him and said to him, "One thing you lack: go and sell all you possess and give to the poor, and you will have treasure in heaven; and come, follow Me." But at these words he was saddened, and he went away grieving, for he was one who owned much property. (Mark 10:17–22 NASB95)

My high school days started out slow and uneventful. I was an average, C student. I liked earning money more than I liked studying. I didn't realize that getting a good education and studying hard would help me earn more money later in life. I read once that earning a high school diploma and obtaining a college degree will earn you $1 million more in life compared to not having them.

The highlight of my day as a sophomore and junior was finishing school at one o'clock. I was part of the early-release student-work program. My first job was working as a busboy cleaning off tables at a local restaurant. During my senior year and continuing on through college, I worked in the mailroom for local bank.

God is very faithful to us and sometimes we don't realize how He works to open doors in life, guiding us along the way. Growing up without a father, God knew that I needed a mentor. God blessed me with several mentors who were outstanding men. During my senior year of high school, a critical period of my life, God placed these remarkable men in front of me.

The first two great men I met were a part of my school project. The title of my project was "How to Become a Successful Leader and Entrepreneur." I interviewed S. Truett Cathy, the founder of Chick-fil-A restaurants, and Andrew Young, mayor of Atlanta.

Mr. Cathy invented the original chicken sandwich. His chicken sandwich recipe was so delicious that he opened successful restaurants across the country. He shared with me his incredible life story and gave me wonderful advice. He was a very godly man and never opened his business on Sunday. He said Sunday was a day for worship and rest. He told me that everyone has three important decisions in life. He called them the three Ms of life. He said make God your master, find a mission to fulfill in life, and select a mate who will be your partner for life. He told me to find my master, my mission, and my mate. Mr. Cathy offered me a job at Chick-fil-A, money for college, and to join him on speaking engagements. We spoke to churches about his life story. After church we returned to his farm south of Atlanta and rode motorcycles. Mr. Cathy was a great cook so we didn't eat Chick-fil-A sandwiches for dinner. Mr. Cathy was a great mentor, and we remained friends throughout his life.

The second remarkable leader that I met was the mayor of Atlanta, Andrew Young. Mayor Young was a historical figure. He was a civil rights leader who marched and worked with Dr. Martin Luther King Jr. He was also a United Nations ambassador. He expanded the Atlanta airport to become the busiest airport in the world. He told me that planning for growth and teamwork were important leadership qualities. He also gave me great financial advice. He said that you can't get rich working for money. You can only get rich when you let your money work for you. That means saving your money and investing your money.

Another mentor who changed my life was Robert Pope. Mr. Pope hired me to work in the bank mailroom. He was the bank president and a very influential member of the community. He told me to set goals for everything that I worked on. Daily goals, monthly goals, and lifetime goals. He told me to always stay positive and not let failure change who you are. He said, "Stay focused on your goals, and you will be successful." He encouraged me to always stay involved in my community and give back to the place I call home. He thought I was a great salesman and encouraged me to be an entrepreneur and start a small business for myself. He said that America is a land of opportunity and that owning a small business can be its greatest reward.

The last two mentors who helped me that year opened the door to a higher education. No member of my family had ever graduated from college, and there was no savings plan available to help me. We were poor, and I accepted the fact that college was not available. Mark Burke and Buddy Truitt were two men who encouraged me to apply for scholarships. Without their help and direction, I would have never attended college. They directly guided me in the application process, and I was accepted into college. Not only did they help me get into college, but they also helped me earn scholarships that paid for everything. I never thought I was smart enough, but with hard work and determination, I graduated from college with honors.

God placed these amazing men in my life that year, which turned out to be my most successful year in high school. My friends and classmates recognized the amazing turnaround that had occurred in my life. I displayed all the characteristics and advice my mentors gave me. My friends at Douglas County High School voted for me to become Mr. Senior Class and Most Likely to Succeed in 1984.

*Douglas County high school principal John Stone and DECA teacher Sandy Wilson join
Bill as he receives a proclamation from Georgia Governor Joe Frank Harris.*

*S. Truett Cathy, founder of Chick-fil-A restaurants was a great motivational
mentor to Bill on finding spiritual guidance and success in life.*

Robert and Virginia Pope were wonderful mentors for Bill. Mr. Pope led Bill to develop goals and make plans for a career in business sales. Bill worked in Robert Pope's bank during high school and college.

Bill met with Atlanta Mayor Andrew Young. Mayor Young explained the importance of teamwork, leadership and successful planning.

Rotary Club President Buddy Truitt congratulates Bill and helped him earn college scholarships to study in Norway and Scotland.

God placed a teacher in my life and introduced me to a student organization that changed my life forever. My high school teacher Sandy Wilson noticed something special in me that others often overlooked. She discovered my hidden abilities and talents that no one else saw. Mrs. Wilson was highly intelligent and motivated with the compassion to help young people. She was not only my teacher but also my DECA advisor. The Distributive Education Clubs of America, DECA, was a national student organization helping young people discover careers in marketing, business, and entrepreneurship. Sandy Wilson was a godly woman who displayed exceptional characteristics that are described in the following Bible verses.

Helping Others

Command them to do good. To be rich and good deeds, and be generous and willing to share. In this way they will lay up treasure for themselves as a firm foundation for the coming age. So that they may take hold of the life that is truly life. (1 Timothy 6:18–19 NIV)

But as for you, brethren, do not grow weary in doing good. (2 Thessalonians 3:13 New King James Version)

The Lord has told you, human, what is good; he has told you what he wants from you: to do what is right to other people, love being kind to others, and live humbly, obeying your God. (Micah 6:8 New Century Version)

And let us not grow weary of doing good, for in due season we will reap, if we do not give up. (Galatians 6:9 ESV)

For it is God which worketh in you both to will and to do of his good pleasure. (Philippians 2:13 King James Version 1900)

Therefore, encourage one another and build one another up, just as you are doing.
(1 Thessalonians 5:11 ESV)

One of the basic principles that formed the DECA club was promoting the American free enterprise system. In January 1984, Mrs. Wilson was teaching our class and helping us prepare a free enterprise project. She was a brilliant marketing planner with ideas to promote free enterprise in our community. Speaking to civic groups, speaking to elementary students, billboards on the highway, proclamations from the government, and displays at small businesses were a part of the strategy. Students were carrying out her mission to learn about free enterprise and promote the free enterprise system. We learned far more helpful life information with this project than simply reading a book.

Mrs. Wilson was always looking for ways to educate her students. A free enterprise rally was taking place in Atlanta and she bought tickets for our class to attend the big event. Business leaders from across the country were going to speak. The keynote speaker was going to be the president of the United States, Ronald Reagan.

When we arrived at the Omni in Atlanta, there were 14,000 people at the free enterprise rally. Our class was a large group and our seats were at the top of the venue in sections ZZ. I had a camera and was in charge of class pictures that day. I told Mrs. Wilson that I wanted to get a picture with President Reagan for the school yearbook. She said that sounded great, but I had over 14,000 people in front of me wanting to do the same thing. That was a big obstacle to overcome. She said, "OK, but check back with me soon because I'm staying with the other students."

I asked myself, "What is the best way to meet a president?" The secret service agents who guard the president seemed to be the best way to get close to him. I noticed a man dressed in a nice suit, wearing sunglasses, and carrying a gun on his belt. I determined that he must be a secret service agent so I went over to talk with him. I said, "Sir, I am a high school student working on a free enterprise project and I would like to meet the president." He said, "Son, I can't help you so move on." I did move down to section W, where I saw another secret service agent. I said, "Sir, I am a member of the DECA club, and I would like to meet the president." He said, "Son, I'm working in this section so I can't help you." I moved on down to section H, where I saw another secret service agent on duty. I said, "Sir, I am a student from Douglas County High School, and I want to meet the president to get a picture for our yearbook." He said, "Son, go down to the front of the stage, where you can take a picture."

I finally arrived at the front of the stage. I was in front of over 14,000 people and worked my way through gun-carrying secret service agents. I turned around to wave at Mrs. Wilson, who was still in sections ZZ, to let her know I made it through all the obstacles. Suddenly, I was surrounded by secret service agents. They looked angry and wanted to know what I was doing. They said, "Who are you, and what are your intentions? We have watched you pass through our checkpoints. You have been very suspicious and our job is to protect the president from people like you." I was so frightened that I was going to be arrested and jailed for my conduct. I said, "Please, please, please, listen to me. I am a harmless DECA student from Douglas County High School working on a free enterprise project. I wanted to get a picture of the president for our yearbook. I am innocent. Please don't arrest me and send me to jail. My teacher is way back there in section ZZ, and she can confirm this information."

The chief secret service agent told me to sit down on the front row and they would deal with me when the program finished. Well, I was still terrified and sat quietly in my seat, fearing the end of the program. The president spoke and many business leaders spoke about our wonderful American free enterprise system. But I was too afraid to pay attention, not knowing what was going to happen to me. I had a great seat, but my mind was in another place.

When the program concluded, the secret service agent returned to my seat and said, "Follow me." I soon realized that I was probably going to jail as we walked to a room behind the stage.

The secret service agent looked at me and said, "Son, good luck with your school project. Now go get that picture you wanted." He opened the door to the room and I was standing face-to-face with the president of the United States. I said, "Mr. President, I am a DECA student who believes in free enterprise and I'm so excited to meet you. My teacher, Mrs. Wilson, is never going to believe I met you, so will you please take a picture of the two of us?" The president said, "I can do better than that. I will have the White House photographer take a picture and send it to your high school."

I couldn't believe that I was standing face-to-face with the most powerful man in the world. Persistence and determination carried the day as I overcame so many obstacles to meet our president. I thanked the president for his excellent leadership and a kind spirit.

I turned eighteen that year and was eligible to vote. Ronald Reagan was the first president I voted for.

Mrs. Wilson wanted to know where I had been, so I told her I met the president. She was so amazed by my story that she knew it had to be true.

A few weeks later, an official package arrived from the White House in Washington, DC. It was that unforgettable picture of President Reagan and me.

After this amazing adventure, I told Mrs. Wilson that I wanted to be the DECA president. She said, "Not only will I help you become the Georgia DECA president, but I will also help you become the national DECA president." She was a brilliant campaign manager, and she was right. I was elected the Georgia DECA president, and the following year, I was elected the national DECA president. This special lady helped me and changed my life forever.

As the national DECA president, Tim Coffey became my national DECA advisor. Mr. Coffey was a wonderful mentor as we traveled to state conventions across the country. From San Francisco to Kansas City to New York, I took my first trip on an airplane.

In 1985 and 1987, I appeared on the Muscular Dystrophy Association Jerry Lewis telethon. The telethon was on national television and lasted for twenty-one and a half hours. Each year it was held over the Labor Day weekend in September in Las Vegas, Nevada. The telethon raised millions of dollars to be used for muscular dystrophy research in an effort to find a cure for this terrible disease. Phone banks were set up across the country so people could call in and make donations. There were also many civic groups who raised money throughout the year and presented their donation during the live TV broadcast. Danceathons, skateathons, and walkathons were some of the civic group fundraisers held across the country. DECA clubs, college fraternities and sororities, and local communities and businesses held fun and exciting events to raise money throughout the year.

I represented DECA and was the national youth chairperson for MDA. My job was to introduce young people, who represented the largest fundraisers, to Jerry Lewis. As host of the telethon, Jerry Lewis recognized each person and accepted their fundraising check on national television. Millions of people across the United States watched the telethon, and it was the highest rated program on television. It was held at the Caesar's Palace hotel in Las Vegas.

Jerry Lewis was a famous Hollywood actor and comedian for many years. Many of his famous friends performed during the show, and it was an endless stream of talented people. The entertainment was fantastic, and people were glued to their television for hours. Every A list actor and Grammy-winning musical talent performed for the show. It was the greatest variety show you could ever experience. Because of my role as national youth chairperson, I was onstage and backstage during the entire telethon. It was the first time in my life that I stayed up all night. I never got sleepy because I was so excited to meet so many famous people. Everyone was so kind, and this was truly an unforgettable experience for a small-town boy like me.

Mr. Coffey was my national DECA advisor and chaperone. We shared in the excitement of meeting so many famous people. Most of the time, we stayed backstage in the commissary waiting for my next appearance to introduce guests to Jerry Lewis. There were several cohosts for the telethon, and they remained backstage with us during their breaks from the show. Jerry Lewis, Sammy Davis Jr., Casey Kasem, and Ed McMahon were with us throughout the telethon. They made Mr. Coffey and me feel so comfortable and welcomed us with kindness. Jerry Lewis always called me by my first name as though he knew me for many years. He was so funny both onstage and offstage with a never-ending performance for everyone around him to enjoy.

Sammy Davis Jr. was the most talented singer I had ever met. He was so friendly and always invited Mr. Coffey and me to sit at his table during our breaks. He had endless stories about his famous friends in the entertainment business; it was fascinating to be in his presence. If you listened to the radio in the 1970s and 1980s, you heard Casey Kasem. Each week he would count down America's top forty songs on his radio show that was broadcast from coast to coast. He was so nice to us and shared some amazing music trivia that we thoroughly enjoyed. Ed McMahon had the greatest laugh I've ever heard. He was so jolly and had a joyful personality. I was a huge fan of *The Tonight Show Starring Johnny Carson* so meeting and spending time with Carson's sidekick and announcer was exciting. The telethon was an amazing experience for me, and I will never forget all of those famous and talented people who made me feel so special.

Mr. Coffey and I had another encounter with a celebrity. He was a famous American singer. The 1985 national DECA conference was held in San Francisco, California. As the national president of our organization, I was master of ceremonies during the conference. Fifteen thousand students from across the country were at the opening ceremony. We wanted to surprise the large crowd, and no one knew who the entertainment would be. National DECA invited my mother to attend the conference, and she was my biggest supporter. We decided to sit the surprise entertainment next to my mother before the show started. She was a huge fan of this entertainer and very happy to be a part of the surprise. The entertainer was very worried that the crowd would not recognize him. I told him not to worry because everyone loved his music. Do you remember these songs? "Puppy Love," "Go Away Little Girl," and "A Little Bit Country, a Little Bit Rock 'n' Roll." I hope you guessed it right. Donny Osmond was our entertainment. When I brought him up onstage, the crowd went wild. They all remembered Donny Osmond. It was a great show, and he was an awesome guy.

1985 was designated by the United Nations as International Youth Year. Mr. Coffey received an invitation from the White House for us to attend a celebration ceremony. This was my first visit to the White House, and the event was spectacular. Youth leaders from across the country gathered in the Rose Garden for a ceremony with President Reagan. Once again, I was face-to-face with one of our greatest presidents. I raised my hand and the president recognized me to speak. I said, "The prosperity and progress of our nation depends on the ability of today's youth to understand and plan for tomorrow's world. People make our country the greatest place on earth."

President Reagan agreed.

President Ronald Reagan Quotes

- If we ever forget that we are One Nation Under God, then we will be a nation gone under.
- We are never defeated unless we give up on God.
- Peace is not absence of conflict; it is the ability to handle conflict by peaceful means.
- We can't help everyone, but everyone can help someone.

President Ronald Reagan and Bill Hembree meet at a Free Enterprise Rally.

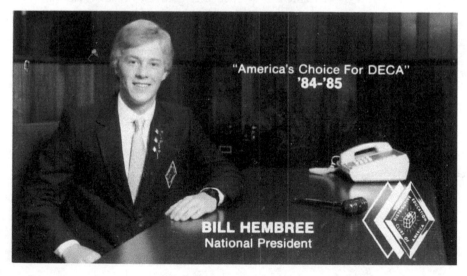

Card used during the National DECA campaign in Kansas City.

DECA teacher Sandy Wilson and Bill celebrate National President victory.

Bill with his high school free enterprise project display.

Tim and Ruth Ellen Coffey with Bill. Tim Coffey was Bill's national DECA advisor and chaperone in the 1980's.

Actor Jerry Lewis with Bill at the muscular dystrophy telethon in Las Vegas.

Singer Donny Osmond with Bill at the National DECA conference in San Francisco.

And then Jesus told them, "Go into all the world and preach the Good News to everyone."
—Mark 16:15 (NLT)

As Christians, we should be disciples of Christ and share the good news of His life with the world. Our Christian character and the way we present ourselves form a model for others to see. My national DECA advisor, Tim Coffey encouraged me to be an exchange student in a foreign country. DECA and the national student exchange group Youth for Understanding developed a partnership. Their mission was to send American students overseas as cultural ambassadors from our country. With Mr. Coffey's help, I received a scholarship to become an exchange student in West Germany.

I didn't speak German and had never visited a foreign country. But as a young American, I was determined to share my life in a nation under God with the world. We are so blessed to live in the greatest nation on earth. God shed His grace on our country and we are a beacon of light and hope for the world. We are one nation, under God, indivisible, with liberty and justice for all.

Now the Lord is the Spirit, and where the Spirit of the Lord is, there is freedom.
(2 Corinthians 3:17 (NIV)

For most people, leaving the comforts of home and venturing out to foreign lands is a frightening idea. A different culture and a different language often seem like barriers that are too great to overcome. When I landed in Germany after crossing the Atlantic Ocean on a Pan-American flight, I was walking by faith alone. Getting lost and the fear of missing my stop created my greatest anxiety as I boarded a train for Frankfurt, Germany. Even though my body was exhausted, I could not fall asleep during the three-hour train ride from Hamburg to Frankfurt. My host family was waiting for me so I could not miss my stop.

The train finally stopped in Frankfurt and I stepped out into a new world. Suddenly, six smiling faces approached me in the train station, and my fears were swept away. Luciano and Ingrid Caminada were my temporary parents and welcomed me to Germany. Their children—Nicole, Kai, Christina, and Michael—also gave me a warm and friendly welcome.

I settled into my new home that was filled with love and happiness. My family back home was large and loving so my new environment was almost the same. My new family was fluent with the English language so I did my best to learn German during my stay.

The United States is separated from most of the world by two large oceans. We sometime take our freedom for granted because we are separated from much of the world. At the time of my visit, Germany was separated into two countries. West Germany was governed on the principles of freedom. East Germany was governed like prisoners under communism and socialism.

We traveled to Berlin, once the capital that was divided after World War II. West Berlin was a thriving city and freedom gave its citizens hope and happiness to live their lives. East Berlin was a dismal city where the government controlled everyone's life. Freedom didn't exist, and there was no hope or happiness. Communism is a godless form of government. I saw hope and no hope in the faces I encountered. As a young American boy, I was truly enlightened and humbled by this trip.

How would you like to be a knight for a night in a one-thousand-year-old German castle? My family told me about this incredible castle that was open to the public as an overnight hotel. Most of the buildings in the United States are relatively new and less than two hundred years old. But in Europe, there are so many buildings that are over one thousand years old and still function for daily use.

I took a train to Oberwesel, Germany, on the Rhine River. High above the town on a mountain overlooking the river was the Castle Schönburg. The castle was said to be haunted and filled with ghostly spirits. I stayed awake most of the night and heard a lot of unusual sounds but saw nothing that would hurt me. My bed and pillow were filled with soft goose feathers. The room was cold and dark just as a castle should be. I explored every room in the castle, including the top of its towering walls and its lowest level, the dungeon. Breakfast and dinner were served in a stately dining room, and I felt like a king. This experience was a wonderful overnight adventure.

My mother raised her family in a Christian home. We attended church every Sunday and deeply engaged with our church family. I didn't know what to expect when I arrived in Germany, but God made sure I was placed in a Christian environment. My host parents, Luciano and Ingrid, were very devout Christians and raise their family in a Christian home. I grew up in the Methodist Church, and my German family was Catholic. The new Catholic rituals that I encountered formed a wonderful learning experience. The foundation and growth of Christianity started with the Roman Catholic Church. My German family and the Catholic Church accepted me with love and compassion. You know that we are all Christians by our love for one another.

Love life.

Love freedom.

Love everyone.

God is love.

The *Caminada family hosted Bill as an exchange student in Frankfurt, Germany.*
Christina, Bill, Ingrid, Kai, Luciano, Nicole and Michael.

Bill stayed at the Schönburg Castle on the Rhine River in Germany.

The fear of the Lord is the beginning of knowledge; fools despise wisdom and instruction.
—Proverbs 1:7 (ESV)

Give instruction to a wise man, and he will be still wiser; teach
a righteous man, and he will increase in learning.
—Proverbs 9:9 (NKJV)

The journey through life is a continuing education process. Every day we are educated, informed, and enlightened by something new. Education never ends, and we should open our minds to information and opportunities that help us grow. I believe the Bible is the starting point for all educational endeavors.

The Bible tells us about four individuals who received a formal education that was equivalent to college today. Moses, Daniel, Solomon, and Paul all took part in a level of higher education. God used their strong education foundation and placed them in positions of influence and power. All wisdom comes from God to carry out His plan for the world.

I was the first member of my family to graduate from college. But the beginning of my journey to gain a college degree was filled with rejection. I was surrounded by teachers and mentors who encouraged me, but my past overshadowed their support. For most of my middle and high school years, I was a very poor student. I was lazy, depressed, unmotivated, and lacked any direction for my future. All this time added up to poor grades and being terrible at taking test. I was a C student with a bad SAT score. Most college admissions offices reviewed my work and determined that I would fail out of college. They rejected me.

The University of Georgia school of business, the University of Georgia school of agriculture, West Georgia College, and Berry College all sent me rejection letters. The only college that I was accepted to was Johnson & Wales University in Providence, Rhode Island. The only reason I was accepted to Johnson & Wales University was because of a man in their admissions office. Mark Burke had worked with me as the national DECA president. He recognized the potential I had for success in college and convinced the admissions board to give me a full-tuition scholarship.

Rhode Island was a faraway place for me, and I never anticipated leaving Georgia to attend college. I knew that I would be homesick, but it was the only opportunity available to continue my education. I packed up my car and said goodbye to my family as I started the 1,200-mile journey to my new college home.

My mother always told me when you move to a new city and feel lonely, find a church. I grew up as a country boy, and being in the city of Providence was a big change for me. I was very lonely. I looked in the local phone book to find a church nearby. A church's advertisement caught my attention. It was the First Baptist Church in America. It was literally the first Baptist church established in the United States. Two hundred years earlier, a man named Roger Williams founded the city of Providence and started his own church. He called it the First Baptist Church.

On Sunday morning, I walked alone from my dormitory to church. I arrived early to this beautiful, old church and sat on the back row. There was a large crowd in attendance that fall day, and the church was full. I no longer felt alone as we sang church hymns and rejoiced together.

Before starting his sermon, the preacher asked that all visitors please stand up. Three people stood up that morning. I stood up on the back row, and another man stood up on the front row. The preacher asked us to introduce ourselves. I said, "My name is Bill Hembree. I am a college student from Winston, Georgia." The guy on the front row said, "Hi, my name is Jimmy Carter. I was president of the United States from Plains, Georgia."

The preacher was very happy to have so many guests from Georgia. The church service was excellent, and after the program finished, I met the former president. We talked for a long time about Georgia, and he was visiting his daughter in college. Go to church, and you never know who you might meet. I met the president and sat in a two-hundred-year-old church. God truly blessed me that day.

My biggest fear about attending college was that I was not smart enough to be there. Failing my classes and losing my scholarship was always on my mind. I knew how to work, but I did not know how to study. The fear of losing such a valuable scholarship motivated me to do my best. I visited all my professors during their office hours and accepted any extra credit work I could find. I was at the college study hall every day, where tutors helped me with my classwork. One of my professors gave me some great advice. He said, "Bill, you have twenty-four hours in a day. Eight hours to study, eight hours to sleep, and eight hours to play." I followed that plan every day and graduated from college with honors. My GPA was 3.57.

In order to pay for my dormitory cost and weekly meal plan, I applied to become a resident assistant. I was hired and the resident assistant position paid for my room and board. The RA job required a lot of responsibilities and leadership roles. I became a counselor and leader for the six hundred students living in my dormitory. College life has many challenges, and I became a counselor for many students. There was nothing boring about being an RA.

Almost every weekend, some student pulled the fire alarm requiring us to evacuate the entire building in the middle of the night. This was always a false alarm but very frustrating for everyone. A group of freshmen boys thought it was entertaining to drop their beanbag chairs from the sixth-floor window and watch them explode when they hit the street. We caught another group of guys pulling a beer keg up the side of the building with the rope from their dorm room. We had a girl who was pregnant and in labor get stuck in the elevator. We had to call the fire department to rescue her, and they delivered the baby successfully.

Life is an educational journey, and the Bible is an educational book delivered to us by God.

> Blessed are those who find wisdom, those who gain understanding. (Proverbs 3:13 NIV)

> The mind of the prudent acquires knowledge, and the ear of the wise seeks knowledge. (Proverbs 18:15 NASB95)

> Moses was educated in all the learning of the Egyptians, and he was a man of power in words and deeds. (Acts 7:22 NASB95)

> God gave Solomon very great wisdom and understanding, and knowledge as vast as the sands of the seashore. (1 Kings 4:29 NLT)

> I thank and praise you, God of my ancestors: You have given me wisdom and power, You have made known to me what we asked of you, You have made known to us the dream of the King. (Daniel 2:23 NIV)

Mark Burke is with his wife Tracey and family. Mark was a college admissions representative and the one who helped Bill get into college with a full tuition scholarship to attend Johnson and Wales University.

Johnson and Wales University President Dr. Morris J.W. Gaebe presents college senior Bill Hembree with President's leadership trophy.

Bill graduated from Johnson and Wales University with a 3.57 GPA and two college degrees in Marketing. Associates degree and Bachelor's degree.

Then Jesus came to them and said, "All authority in heaven and on earth has been given
to me. Therefore, go and make disciples of all nations, baptizing them in the name of
the Father and the Son and of the Holy Spirit, and teaching them to obey everything I
have commanded you. And surely, I am with you always, to the very end of the age."
—Matthew 28:18–20 (NIV)

When I was a little boy, I dreamed of sailing around the world. The earth looks like a beautiful blue marble from space. Over 70 percent of the Earth's surface is covered by its vast oceans of water. I wanted to be like those famous seafaring explorers that I read about in my history book. Christopher Columbus and Ferdinand Magellan were my favorite explorers. They crossed the great oceans in search of new discoveries that would change the world.

As I was changing classes one day during college, I noticed an intriguing flyer on the wall outside my classroom. It said, "See the world on semester at sea." I couldn't believe that there was an organization that owns a ship and took college students to study around the world. I contacted the Institute for Shipboard Education to find out more about their program. It was true. A very old cruise ship had been converted into a college environment that sailed around the world. You would cross three great oceans and visit twelve countries earning college credit by taking classes on the ship. I was determined to go on semester at sea, but how would I pay for it? There was an opportunity for poor students like me. I earned a scholarship and participated in a work program on the ship.

Our ship, named the *SS Universe,* set sail from Vancouver, Canada. We were crossing the Pacific Ocean, the largest ocean in the world, on our way to Japan. We encountered violent storms with thirty-foot waves crashing against the ship. The constant motion caused most of us to get seasick. In the middle of the Pacific Ocean, we crossed the international date line as we traveled westward. We had to change our clocks and calendars because we lost an entire day. We had professors who taught our classes every day on the ship.

It took fourteen days to cross the Pacific Ocean.

We finally arrived in Japan. We were only in the country for a few days and had to complete field studies as part of the education program. I chose to travel to the town of Hiroshima. I boarded a bullet train from the port city, and it traveled at 120 miles per hour. I had never in my life moved so quickly on the ground. We quickly arrived in Hiroshima. I wanted to write a paper about this historical city. In hopes of ending World War II and saving American lives, the American president, Harry Truman, ordered the first atomic bomb to be dropped. The atomic bomb was so powerful and destructive that Japan surrendered and the war was over. I was standing in the Hiroshima Museum that displayed the horrible images of human death caused by the atomic bomb. Japanese students surrounded me, but there was no anger or hostility directed at me. A classmate and I were the only Americans present that day. The Japanese students offered us love and kindness and were grateful for our visit. They only wanted peace and hope for our future.

The next country we sailed to was Taiwan. As a young, devout Christian growing up in Georgia, I was not exposed to other religions. When our ship arrived in Asia, I noticed two things: large populations of people and a different religion from Christianity. Buddhism was the first religion I encountered. Buddhists believe that the human life is one of suffering and that meditation, spiritual and physical labor, and good behavior are the ways to achieve enlightenment or nirvana.

Our next stop was the Chinese city of Hong Kong. We visited a community called Aberdeen. This is a community on water where hundreds of boats are tied together to provide housing for its people. Thousands of people spend their entire lives on these boats called junks. They fish every day to provide for their families. I didn't notice any religion in the Chinese society during my visit. The most populated country in the world was focused on work and business.

We visited two more countries: the Philippines and Malaysia. Large populations in the cities of Manila and Singapore were contrasted by rural jungles.

The next country we visited in Asia was India. Our ship docked in the city of Bombay. You are overwhelmed by the large number of people living in this country. As part of our field study, we visited the home of Gandhi, who started the movement of nonviolent protest. The most common religion in India is Hinduism. Hindus believe in the continuous cycle of life, death, and reincarnation. They also believe in karma, the universal law of cause and effect. One of the key thoughts of Hinduism is atman or the belief in soul. This philosophy holds that each living creature has a soul, and they're all part of the supreme soul.

Our ship then sailed across the Indian Ocean and into the Red Sea to the country of Egypt. We visited the city of Cairo on the Nile River. Our field study included a trip to see the ancient pyramids and tour the Cairo Museum. The museum was filled with artifacts from pharaohs like Tutankhamen and Ramses. The amount of gold and jewelry they possessed was spectacular. Five-thousand-year-old statues and obelisks showed the incredible craftsmanship of the ancient Egyptians.

I had three unforgettable adventures while in Egypt. I climbed up the largest pyramid and walked into the pharaoh's burial chamber inside. I also walked around the Sphinx and the other two large pyramids. One day I rode a camel across the Egyptian desert, and the next day, I rode an Arabian horse back across the desert to Cairo.

The next port city we visited was Istanbul, Turkey. This ancient city was once called Constantinople. It was named for the Roman emperor Constantine, who proclaimed that Christianity was the official religion of the Roman Empire two thousand years ago. Islam is the most common religion in the Middle East today. The followers of Islam are called Muslims. Muslims are monotheistic and worship an all-knowing God who in Arabic is known as Allah. Followers of Islam came to live a life of complete submission to Allah. They believe that nothing can happen without Allah's permission, but humans have free will. We visited the Muslim religious site called the Blue Mosque in Istanbul. It was built by the Roman emperor Constantine two thousand years ago as his royal palace. We also visited the ancient city of Troy, which is in Turkey. Greek mythology tells the story of the war between Greece and Troy. Greek soldiers hid in a wooden Trojan horse that was carried into Troy so they could rescue their queen Helen. It was November, so we celebrated Thanksgiving in the country of Turkey.

Our ship then sailed across the Mediterranean Sea and the Black Sea to reach the Soviet Union. Today we call most of this area of the world Russia. The Soviet Union was the foundation of communism and socialism in the world. It was completely opposite of the democratic republic we live in. The Soviet Union was once called the Evil Empire and was involved with a Cold War with the Western democracies.

There was no level of freedom in this country, and the secret government police called the KGB spied on you every day. The students we met at the local university were trapped in this communist country. They had no hope, they had no freedom, they were lost, and their future looked bleak. I wanted to help them escape the misery of this totalitarian government. I wanted them to experience the freedom and opportunities we have in the United States.

1987 marked the two hundredth anniversary of the United States Constitution. The Constitution is the foundation of our republic. Our freedom is based on government of the people, by the people, and for the people. Before I left on semester at sea, I was selected to serve on the Bicentennial Constitution celebration committee. I handed out pocket-sized copies to schools in my community. This little book was a reminder to everyone on why we are a free country. I carried fifty copies with me on the ship so I could share them with the people of the world.

The Soviet Union considered the United States Constitution as pure propaganda. I would have been arrested and placed in jail if I had been caught with copies of the Constitution. I decided to take a chance because freedom is worth fighting for. I had ten copies of the pocket-sized Constitution in the secret compartment inside my camera case. There was a KGB checkpoint on the dock as we left the ship each day. They always asked where we were going and who we were going to see. They also checked our backpacks and bags for illegal material. Even though I was terrified on the inside, I was cool and calm on the outside. God was with me as I told the secret agent that I was going to speak at the university and take a group picture with my camera. He didn't open the secret compartment in my camera case that held the constitutions. He gave me an OK and sent me forward through the gates.

I gave all ten copies to the wonderful students that I had met at the university. They were all English majors and were looking forward to reading this amazing document. Their minds were filled with hope and excitement that didn't exist before. I love freedom, I love my country, and I love my God. The risk of being arrested was a risk worth taking so I could make a difference in our world.

We left the Soviet Union and our ship sailed to Dubrovnik, Yugoslavia. We then crossed the Mediterranean Sea to Cadiz, Spain. We visited the Rock of Gibraltar and the university town of Granada, Spain.

It took ten days to cross the Atlantic Ocean on our way home to Fort Lauderdale, Florida. We traveled 23,000 miles across three oceans, visiting four continents, twelve countries, and twenty time zones. We arrived home on Christmas Eve. Homecoming was the best Christmas present ever!

In 1987 Bill traveled around the world on this ship as a Semester at Sea student.

After a fourteen-day journey to cross the Pacific Ocean, Bill's ship arrived in Japan.

Egypt was one of Bill's favorite countries to visit as he circled the globe. He took this picture during sunrise at the Great Pyramid of Giza.

Bill used his video camera to capture pictures while visiting ruins at the ancient city of Troy in the country of Turkey.

I have always believed that the best way to change the world or enjoy the world and its beauty is to see it firsthand. A picture alone cannot describe or express God's perfect creation that we call earth. Live and be grateful for each day that we are given. Travel and seek adventures that will give you a rich educational reward. I earned a college scholarship to study at the international summer school sponsored by the University of Oslo in Norway.

Norway is called the land of the midnight sun. It is one of the few populated places on earth where sunset merges into sunrise, with no darkness in between. During the summer, Norway experiences twenty-four hours of daylight. Each day the sun crosses the sky and never sets below the horizon. The Norwegian people are energized with celebrations and excitement over these endless summer days. Activities go on around the clock as people enjoy the light and warm sunshine.

June 21 is a National Day of Celebration in Norway with the beginning of summer. It is a time to sing, dance, and be merry with festivals around the country. The food and activities are enjoyed by everyone. My favorite dish was a blueberry porridge dessert. I stayed awake for twenty-four hours that day and never seemed to get tired. The sunshine was always there and acted like a beacon of energy. It is a unique feeling to experience light all through the day with no darkness ever falling across the earth.

My Norwegian friends took me swimming in a nearby lake. It was summertime and the days were warm so I looked forward to a nice swim. Unfortunately, the air was warm but the water was freezing cold. I didn't last very long in the water, but my friends told me that swimming in the Norwegian lake makes you an honorary Viking. One of the families that I lived with for a short time was nudist a few hours each day. They soaked up the sun and were carefree. They respected my conservative ideas and never asked me to join them. I was happy to stay inside the house and take a nap while they enjoyed the sunshine.

I studied Norwegian history and political science at the University of Oslo that summer. My professor was Arne Olav Brundtland. He was the prime minister of Norway's husband. He was a great teacher and the class was fascinating and filled with his stories of being inside the political world. We also studied the Vikings and their expansion across Europe during a period called the Dark Ages. The Vikings worshiped pagan gods and their warriors terrorized Christian communities. The Vikings were excellent sailors, and their longboats enabled them to make raids on coastal villages. They valued gold and silver and would kill mercilessly anyone who challenged them. Between AD 700 and 1000, the Vikings undertook large-scale raiding, colonizing, conquest, and trading throughout Europe. Many Christians feared the world was ending and referred to this time as the Dark Ages. Today Norway is a Christian nation filled with the light of the world.

> Then Jesus again spoke to them, saying," I am the Light of the world; he who follows Me will not walk in the darkness, but will have the Light of life." (John 8:12 NASB95)

While I am in the world, I am the Light of the world. (John 9:5 NIV)

> I have come as light into the world, so that everyone who believes in Me will not remain in darkness. (John 12:46 NASB95)

Believers in Jesus Christ will someday have eternal light in Heaven as it says in the book of Revelations, "There will be no more night. They will not need the light of a lamp or the light of the sun, for the Lord God will give them light. And they will reign for ever and ever." (Revelations 22:5 NIV)

The Lord is my shepherd; I shall not want.
He makes me to lie down in green pastures:
He leads me beside still waters.
He restores my soul: he leads me in the paths of righteousness for his name's sake.
Even though I walk through the valley of the shadow of
death, I will fear no evil: for you are with me;
your rod and your staff, they comfort me.
You prepare a table before me in the presence of my enemies: you anoint my head with oil;
my cup overflows.
Surely goodness and mercy shall follow me all the days of my life:
and I shall dwell in the house of the Lord forever.
—Psalm 23:1–6 (ESV)

I was very fortunate to earn a Rotary Club international scholarship to study at the University of Glasgow, Scotland. Living in Europe for a year gave me a base to travel across the continent. Trains are the most efficient way to travel in Europe, so I bought a very cheap Eurail Train Pass. Scotland was my new home, and I made plans to travel to a different European country during each school break.

My mother's last name was Buchanan, which is a Scottish clan. There are many castles in Scotland that served as home to Scottish clans or families. MacDonald, Campbell, MacKenzie, MacIntosh, MacLeod, Gordon, Robertson, and Stewart are just a few of the many clans. My favorite towns in Scotland were Edinburgh, St. Andrews, and Aberdeen. The most beautiful place was the Island of Skye.

One adventure took me to the town of Inverness, which is on the shore of Loch Ness. I have always been fascinated with unsolved mysteries. Many years ago, a picture was taken of a dinosaur-looking creature swimming across the lake. It was called the Loch Ness monster. No other evidence was ever found of the Loch Ness monster, but the mystery created a lot of interest. My friends and I took a boat across the lake in search of the monster. After a day of searching, we found nothing.

Back in the town of Inverness, I stopped at a pub to ask the locals about the Loch Ness monster. A local gentlemen told me, "Son, let me tell you how to find the Loch Ness monster and see it with your own eyes. You need to buy a bottle of single malt Scotch whiskey." Glenfiddich and Glenmorangie were his two favorite drinks. "Wait until midnight and go to Urquhart Castle on the lake. Drink the entire bottle of whiskey, and I will guarantee that you will see the Loch Ness monster." I decided not to do that, so the mystery still exists.

Another great Scottish tradition honors the famous poet Robert Burns. Burns Night is a wonderful event filled with dancing, reading poetry, and eating Scottish food. The most famous dish in Scotland is haggis. Haggis is a sheep's heart, liver, and lungs cooked together inside a sheep's stomach. I made it through dinner, but I can tell you that I have no desire to try haggis ever again.

My favorite country in Europe is Italy. Its famous cities, history, and delicious food make it a wonderful place to visit. Rome is my favorite city because of its ancient history. The Colosseum and the Forum are amazing sites to see. Julius Caesar, Caesar Augustus, Marcus Aurelius, and Hadrian are just a few of the famous Roman emperors. Early Christians were persecuted in the Roman Empire, but in AD 313, Emperor Constantine made Christianity the official religion.

The apostle Peter and the apostle Paul preached about the good news of Jesus Christ in the city of Rome. They were both arrested, imprisoned, and crucified in Rome. The foundation of the Catholic Church is called the Vatican. Peter was crucified at its central point called St. Peter's Basilica. A short distance away is the site where Paul was crucified, called St. Paul's Basilica. These two men were critical figures in the growth of Christianity.

St. Peter's Basilica is one of the most beautiful churches in the world. As a young Christian, I was inspired to worship and pray in this magnificent building. I am not Catholic, but I thought it was important to pray with the priest. I was young and alone in a faraway country. I needed spiritual support and encouragement as I traveled alone.

I entered one of the many confessional booths inside St. Peter's Basilica. I wasn't sure what to say, but I asked the priest to pray for me. I wanted to remain safe and in good health as I traveled each day. I told the priest I was an exchange student from the United States and I didn't speak Italian. I told him about my family back home and my Christian faith. I updated him on my journey from Scotland to Italy. I told him how grateful I was to spend time in this beautiful church. I felt an overwhelming amount of peace and comfort during my prayer.

The priest never said anything, so I thanked him for his time and said goodbye. I thought that maybe he did not speak English. When I left the confessional booth, I noticed a sign hanging on the side. The sign was written in Italian so I asked another priest walking by what it said. He said, "The sign says, 'Gone to lunch.' This booth is empty."

Well, I was a little embarrassed about giving a confessional in an empty booth. No worries. The presence of God was with me, and my prayers were heard and answered.

Venice is another beautiful city in Italy. Canals and waterways connect the city as water roads.

Gondolas and other boats can carry you around town. In my opinion, Venice is one of the most romantic cities in the world. Couples can take gondola rides to enjoy delicious food at restaurants or enjoy the quiet serenity of floating around town. St. Mark's Basilica and Square are nice places to visit. The Rialto Bridge connects you with boutique shopping and nice hotels. I was alone during my visit but dreamed of one day returning for a romantic trip with my wife.

Florence is another remarkable Italian town. It is the capital of Italy's Tuscany region. It is home to many masterpieces of Renaissance art and architecture and the favorite city for many American tourist. A cathedral called the Duomo has a terra-cotta tiled dome that is visible from around the city. Michelangelo is one of the city's most famous artists. His most famous sculpture, called *David*, is a masterpiece. I sat in the museum for over an hour admiring the amazing work by Michelangelo. I was also mesmerized by his perfect painting on the roof of the Sistine Chapel in Rome.

One of the most unusual buildings I have ever seen is the leaning Tower of Pisa. The town of Pisa, Italy, is very charming. But you can't take your eyes off the leaning bell tower. It looks like it's going to fall any minute. It was built in the year 1372 so it will probably remain standing for a long time to come. I climbed the interior steps to the top of the building. I then walked outside of each level to feel the sensation of the leaning tower. There were no rails to hold onto so it was a thrilling walk.

In my opinion, one of the most beautiful cities in Europe is Lucerne, Switzerland. The picturesque city sits on Lake Lucerne amid snowcapped mountains of the Swiss Alps. The view is truly breathtaking. The Jesuit church and the Chapel Bridge are surrounded by medieval buildings.

Salzburg, Austria, is another mountain town that is worth the visit. The city was home to Wolfgang Amadeus Mozart, one of the most famous musicians in history.

One of the most emotional experiences of my life occurred in the city of Amsterdam, Netherlands. I read the diary of Anne Frank in middle school and was deeply moved by her story. She was an innocent, young girl caught in the tragedy of World War II. I visited the hiding place in Amsterdam where her family lived for two years to escape Nazi death camps. Sadly, in the end, they were found and captured. Anne Frank died in a Nazi death camp. Standing in that tiny room where she wrote her diary was an unforgettable experience for me. Her life was gone, but her words inspired us all.

Paris, France, is the most visited city in Europe and is known as the city of lights. The Eiffel Tower and the Louvre Museum are the biggest landmarks in Paris. Most people want to see the portrait of *Mona Lisa* by Leonardo da Vinci, but you can spend days seeing all the other exhibits in the museum. My two favorite places in Paris are churches. The Sacre-Coeur is the most beautiful basilica sitting high on a hill above the city. It is surrounded by starving artists displaying their work. It is a perfect place to sit down and enjoy the beauty of Paris. Notre Dame Cathedral is another beautiful church. The architecture of the building is stunning. The stained-glass windows in the cathedral are absolutely beautiful. Looking at the windows while sitting in the church gives you a spiritual encounter and opportunity for prayer that is a very memorable experience. I will dwell in the house of the Lord forever.

Bill speaks to Rotary Clubs in Scotland as part of his college exchange student program at the University of Glasgow.

While attending college and living in Germany, Norway and Scotland, Bill traveled by train to visit many countries in Europe. This was a trip to Paris, France.

Love is patient, love is kind. It does not envy, it does not boast, it is not proud.
It does not dishonor others, it is not self-seeking, it is not easily angered, it
keeps no record of wrongs. Love does not delight in evil but rejoices with the
truth. It always protects, always trusts, always hopes, always perseveres.
—1 Corinthians 13:4–7 (NIV)

On Christmas Eve in 1990, I got down on my knee and asked Elizabeth Mozley Camp to marry me. I wanted to propose on a billboard or with an airplane in the sky, but I was broke. I had just finished college and borrowed $2,000 from the bank to buy the wedding ring. We had a six-month engagement and paid for the wedding on our own. It was surprising to me, but we had to pay $1,000 to rent the church. At 7 p.m. on Saturday, June 22, 1991, Beth and I were married at the First Methodist Church in Douglasville, Georgia.

We have been married for over thirty years and our love for one another is the foundation of our marriage. I fell in love with Beth the first time I saw her in high school. I was in love with her beauty; it was love at first sight. I love her more and more each day. I will love her forever, until the end of time.

Beth is my partner in life. God never intended for us to be alone, and in the beginning, He created man and woman. I am never lonely when Beth is near me. She is my partner in everything we do, and together we are a solid team. Fear and uncertainty are swept away when she is by my side.

Beth is a wonderful mother. She gives unconditional love to her children. She nurtured and guided our three sons to grow into responsible men. She runs our household with daily responsibilities to keep our world in order. The love she has for her children is present and everlasting. She gives our sons a tender love and protects them from a dangerous world. Her warm and loving heart has touched the souls of our sons. Nothing will ever break the bond between her and her children.

Beth is a great parent. The role of a parent can be very challenging. All of our children are unique and very different from one another. Her role as a parent is sometimes played differently with each child. Children also face many challenges, and it becomes a parent's role to guide the different personalities. Beth disciplined our sons when it was needed. She also enforced a daily routine and gave our sons a structured life to follow.

Beth is my best friend. She is a friend I can always count on, in good times and bad times. She is a friend who will lift my spirits when I am sad. Her smile makes me happy and brightens my day. I seek her advice every day, and she helps me with decisions I could not face alone.

I have a physical attraction to Beth. She is stunningly beautiful. I love to hold her, kiss her, hug her, and touch her every day. This physical connection makes our bond stronger. We are emotionally connected together with passion and love.

Beth and I are both Christians. This is important to us because we share the same religious beliefs. Our faith brings us together every day. We worship together and celebrate our blessings. Our faith also holds us together when bad things occur in our lives. We believe in one God. We also believe that Jesus Christ is the only mediator between God and man. You must have a spiritual life with your wife to gain peace and understanding against the darkness of our world.

I respect Beth for who she is and what she does with her life. Respect is very important in a relationship. If you respect someone, you are less likely to get involved in arguments. Respect is more powerful than anger, hatred, and jealousy. If you love someone, you should respect them.

Another important factor that helps our marriage work is that we share common goals. We make financial decisions together. We are both frugal and work hard to spend money wisely to meet our daily needs. We save our money and live modestly. We openly talk about our family goals, our personal goals, our work goals, and our spending goals. Open discussions help us stay on target with our desires and avoid unnecessary surprises.

Beth and I both have a very strong work ethic. We are not lazy people. Hard work was instilled in us by our parents, and we accept our daily responsibilities to get our jobs done.

We each had a very modest childhood living in very similar conditions. We both experienced the same struggles with limited resources. This common background keeps us grounded so that we live within our means. It is easier to make decisions for the future when you can relate to conditions from the past.

We both love people, especially children and babies. We love to engage family and friends and are fulfilled with spending time together. Birthdays and holidays are especially rewarding. Connecting with people energizes us and stimulates an emotional connection. There's nothing more special than being a part of a child's life. Children bring joy and happiness to us. They fill our hearts with love and compassion.

Beth and I support each other's interests. Sometimes our interests are the same, but many times our interests are different. It is OK to be different and to enjoy different things in life. Don't be resentful in your differences, but rejoice and celebrate with the person you love.

Our love for music is one of our strongest connections. Music unlocks our emotions and gives us great satisfaction. We love to attend concerts so we can experience live music. The musicians, the lyrics, and the sound allow us to escape and release our emotions. Music helps us relax and forget the challenges of each day.

Beth is a great companion and my strongest advocate in life. She will always fight for me and defend me from my enemies.

Beth is kind. She treats people nicely and is always willing to help a friend. She greeted everyone with a smile no matter who you are or where you come from. She has a tender heart and is respectful to everyone.

Beth is a good listener. She knows when it is time to talk and time to listen. When it is time to listen, she gives her undivided attention. She is supportive, helpful, and understanding.

Beth has a positive attitude. We live in a world filled with anger and hatred, but she finds the good in our world. She is not filled with negative energy, but she is alive with positive thoughts.

Beth is a compassionate caregiver. When I was sick and weak, she made me strong. She is the greatest cook I have ever known. Her love for baking and cooking is a great reward for my sons and me. Everyone loves the food she cooks, and her recipes are outstanding. My mother told me that the closest way to a man's heart was through his stomach. Beth is a cooking master, and those who have the pleasure of enjoying her meals are truly blessed. The dishes she cooks are delicious, tasty, and delightful.

I love spending time with Beth. As long as we are together, I am happy. Sitting quietly next to each other or taking a short walk, it doesn't matter because the time is a special time. When she is away, I miss her presence and her touch. I like to talk to her and listen to her. I like to look at her and kiss her. She makes me proud and happy. She fills my life with joy, and I'm so blessed to call her my wife.

There are three strong women in the Bible who remind me of Beth. The first is Mary, the mother of Jesus. She gave birth to our Savior and is the most remarkable mother who ever lived. Beth is a great mother and adores her sons. Beth reminds me of Rachel, who patiently waited to marry Jacob, the man she truly loved. Beth was patient with me and has rewarded my life with her love. Elizabeth, the lady God blessed to give birth to John the Baptist. The man who told the world of its coming Savior, Jesus Christ. My Elizabeth has changed my world with her endless love.

Beth Hembree my high school sweetheart. 11th grade class picture.

Beth and Bill at the Douglas County high school prom.

Beth and Bill at Beth's Douglas County high school graduation in 1985.

Beth and Bill Hembree on their wedding day, June 22, 1991.

Our first Christmas together as a married couple at our first home in Douglasville, Georgia. Beth, Bill, and our pets, Daisy the dog and Lilly the cat.

Tell us, then, what you think. Is it lawful to pay taxes to Caesar, or not? But Jesus, aware
of their malice, said, "Why put me to the test, you hypocrites? Show me the coin for
the tax." And they brought him a denarius. And Jesus said to them, "Whose likeness
and inscription is this?" They said, "Caesar's." Then he said to them, "Therefore render
to Caesar the things that are Caesar's, and to God the things that are God's."
—Matthew 22:17–21 (ESV)

I have been fascinated with politics for most of my life. The most intriguing aspect is the power
of a politician to change the world for good. Helping people and making a difference in your
community are rewarding endeavors. The Bible tells us to pray for our leaders and that God puts
people in power to accomplish His plans.

I have always believed that one person can make a difference in our world. I grew up as a poor
kid and never understood the power of money. I did study history though and saw where someone
could rise from obscurity and be elected president of the United States. It was very remarkable that
as a young man I met three presidents. My fate allowed me to talk with President Ronald Reagan,
President Jimmy Carter, and President George Bush. All the meetings with the presidents inspired
me to be a candidate and run for public office. I had been elected by students to be president of the
youth organization. So I felt strongly that I could be elected by all the people and make the world
a better place to live.

In order to get elected and start changing the world, you must first win an election. Political
campaigns are exciting and discouraging. Speeches, campaign rallies, and gaining support from
voters with your ideas is exciting and very rewarding. But your political opponents can attack your
ideas and reputation with negative advertising that is very discouraging. The only way to overcome
these political assaults is to stay positive and focus on your message to the voters.

You can't win an election without supporters. Your strongest supporters must be your family.
Beth and my boys were always my biggest fans and hardest working campaigners. Beth and I
endured a lot of unforgettable adventures while campaigning door-to-door. One day we were chased
by dogs and escaped by jumping on top of the car. Another day we were locked in a garage because

I pressed the garage door opener instead of the doorbell. Another day Beth fell off the front porch and landed in the bushes. People often thought that we were Jehovah's Witnesses so they wouldn't open the door to meet us. We always walked in the local parades during the grueling summer heat and were exhausted for days.

At the age of twenty-six, I was elected to the Georgia House of Representatives. I was reelected eight times and served in this distinguished body for eighteen years. I'm very proud of my accomplishments while serving in the General Assembly and believe my efforts made a positive difference for my community and the people of Georgia.

I've always been an advocate of public libraries. I believe a library book that is free to check out can open the door to a better education for the one who reads the book. Part of my district was in a rural area and the nearest library was many miles away. Many people in my district were missing out on the opportunity to enjoy all the library has to offer. I served on the Appropriations Committee in the House of Representatives and secured a $2 million state grant to build the Dog River Library in South Douglas County. I also believe that a solid education can change a young person's life. Vocational education is sometimes better than the traditional education for certain students. Learning trade skills that are used every day in the business world and develop opportunities for a nontraditional student. I secured a $4 million state grant to build the Career Academy at West Georgia Technical College in Douglasville.

While serving government, my supporters called me the "taxpayers' friend." Sometimes taxes can be excessive and detrimental to the people. Many senior citizens in my area lived on a fixed income and were burdened by overtaxation. I passed a law to give Douglas County senior citizens a full exemption from school taxes at the age of sixty-two. This was tax relief for a group of people whose children had left the school system many years earlier. It was taxation with no representation.

Honoring the veterans who fought to protect our country is very important. We owe our freedom to these noble warriors. I changed the name of Bankhead Highway to Veterans Memorial Highway to honor our veterans. I also passed legislation to create memorial bridges for State Representative Tom Kilgore and State Representative Alpha Fowler.

I cosponsored a bill that saved taxpayers $40 million by abolishing the sales tax on private or person-to-person sales of used cars. I was also the author of legislation that became law to allow classic car owners to use original license plates from the 1940s, 1950s, 1960s, and 1970s on refurbished classic cars.

I also passed a law that help blind children receive instruction in braille, so they could read and write at the same level as their peers. I cosponsored a bill that saved school boards millions by exempting them from county and city assessment fees for building new schools.

As chairman of the Higher Education Committee, I worked with the Board of Regents to open Georgia Highlands College in Douglas County. I have a passion for helping others receive a better education so I passed a law to allow part-time college students to receive tuition equalization grants.

I also passed legislation to protect the prestigious HOPE scholarship for future generations. I created a new law called the Foster Child Education Grant. This grant helps kids in state foster care to pay for college expenses like books, tuition, room, and board. I authored a new law to expand student loan programs for Georgia students. I passed House Bill 332 that allows high school students to enroll in a technical college or traditional college and receive the HOPE scholarship to pay their tuition. I also worked with the Board of Regents to allow international baccalaureate students to enter college as sophomores with good test scores. I passed a law to allow homeschool students to earn the HOPE scholarship as starting freshmen if they score in the 85th percentile on the SAT or ACT test.

A young baseball player was hit in the chest with a baseball and died from a heart attack. Football players and runners in afterschool programs have died from heart attacks. Those deaths may have been prevented by the presence of heart defibrillators. I passed a law that requires heart defibrillators in all public school sports programs in Georgia. They are paid for by the American Heart Association and state grants. The Georgia Association of Emergency Medical Services presented me with the Star of Life award for putting defibrillators in schools. The American Heart Association gave me the chain of survival legislative award for saving young people's lives. I also passed a law to help motorcycle riders. House Bill 1392 increases the penalties for motorists who injure or kill motorcycle riders.

I passed legislation to give organ donors a $10,000 tax exemption. This lifesaving law earned me an award from the Georgia Organ Donor Association.

I was the House of Representatives sponsor of the state constitutional amendment that defined marriage.

While serving on the Appropriations Committee, I was always looking for funding to help my community. State grants are available to everyone but require a lot of time and energy to get approval. I became a grant application expert and secured funding for many programs. I secured a $40,000 state grant to improve the local 911 system. I secured a $20,000 state grant to purchase a new computer lab and library equipment for our public schools. I secured a $10,000 state grant to buy imaging equipment for our local fire department. I secured a $7,000 state grant for emergency medical services. I secured two $10,000 grants for local elementary schools to build student walking tracks. I also secured another $10,000 grant to build an outdoor lunch pavilion at a local elementary school. I obtained a $10,000 state grant to help build the Freedom Island Memorial in remembrance of 9/11/2001. I also secured a $10,000 state grant for the local senior citizen center.

Political success comes from good ideas and the determination to turn those ideas into reality by creating new laws that help people. The political process can be very difficult but also very rewarding. Working with people in the community to make things better in our daily lives is a great accomplishment. Ted Davidson served as my campaign manager during the eighteen years I served in state government. Ted is a true patriot and loves his state and country. Together we plotted a course to find victory in each election. His hard work and dedication to my campaigns made our efforts successful.

I won eight reelection campaigns for the Georgia House of Representatives and served in that body for eighteen years. But I was not always successful in my political endeavors. I lost my race to become speaker of the House of Representatives. I also lost political campaigns for the Public Service Commission, the State Senate, and the United States Congress.

As a young legislator in my early twenties, my goal was to change the world and make it a better place. I wasn't successful in changing the world, but I did make a small contribution to make things better.

I received a tremendous honor from the state of Georgia for all of my hard work as a state representative. The General Assembly passed a resolution designating the Bill Hembree Bridge. State Senator Mike Dugan introduced the resolution designating the Bill Hembree Bridge. This wonderful tribute was passed by the State Senate and State House of Representatives. Governor Brian Kemp signed the resolution into law. The bridge is located on State Highway 166 in Douglas County. The bridge crosses the beautiful Dog River Reservoir located in the southern part of the county. My wife, Beth, and my sister, Arubra, developed the idea during my battle with cancer and presented the proposal to the government officials.

Bill Hembree meets President George H.W. Bush and First Lady Barbara Bush

Bill Hembree meets President Jimmy Carter at the First Baptist Church in Providence, Rhode Island.

Beth and Bill at the July 4, 1992 salute to America parade.

Bill Hembree for State Representative campaign supporters on July 4, 1992.

Bill Hembree was elected as a Georgia State Representative on Tuesday November 3, 1992.

Bill Hembree takes the oath of office at the Georgia State Capitol.

Bill Hembree serves as the Grand Marshal for the Shriners Labor Day parade.

Bill Hembree gives a speech to voters at a campaign rally.

Ted Davidson served as Bill's campaign manager. They won nine elections together.

The Georgia General Assembly designated the Bill Hembree Bridge to honor Bill for his hard work, dedication and legislative success helping his community and the people of Georgia.

Jabez cried out to the God of Israel, "Oh, that you would bless me and
enlarge my territory! Let your hand be with me, and keep me from harm
so that I will be free from pain." And God granted his request.
—1 Chronicles 4:10 (NIV)

All hard work brings a profit, but mere talk leads only to poverty.
—Proverbs 14:23 (NIV)

Commit your actions to the Lord, and your plans will succeed.
—Proverbs 16:3 (NLT)

May the favor of the Lord our God rest on us; establish the work of
our hands for us: yes, establish the work of our hands.
—Psalm 90:17 (NIV)

For I know the plans I have for you, declares the Lord, plans to prosper
you and not to harm you, plans to give you hope and a future.
—Jeremiah 29:11 (NIV)

Pay careful attention to your own work, for then you will get the
satisfaction of a job well done, and you won't need to compare yourself to
anyone else. For we are each responsible for our own conduct.
—Galatians 6:4–5 (NLT)

Whatever you do, work at it with all your heart, as working for the Lord, not for human masters.
—Colossians 3:23 (NIV)

The hardworking farmer should be the first to receive a share of the crops.
—2 Timothy 2:6 (NIV)

By the seventh day God had finished the work He had been doing; so, on the seventh
day He rested from all His work. Then God blessed the seventh day and made it
holy, because on it He rested from all the work of creating that He had done.
—Genesis 2:2–3 (NIV)

For I can do everything through Christ, who gives me strength.
—Philippians 4:13 (NLT)

God intended for us to work and be engaged in this world. We will continue to work in the kingdom of heaven to glorify our everlasting God. I have been blessed with a career in insurance sales and management for over twenty years. Every day my job gives me the satisfaction of helping people. My business protects people from catastrophic events that occur in our world. Automobile accidents, house fires, and unexpected death can have devastating effects on you and your family. Our insurance agency provides you with protection and peace of mind regarding the things that are most valuable in your life.

My first job in high school was working as a busboy at a local restaurant. This job introduced me to the reward of a paycheck and the camaraderie of coworkers. My second job was working at a local bank during high school and college. My primary role was working in the mailroom, but each week, I was called to be an emergency cash carrier. The bank branches would often run short on cash. So I delivered bags of cash from the main office to the bank branches in other communities. On one occasion, I transported $30,000 cash all alone in my 1978 Pontiac Grand Prix. That is a big responsibility for a teenager, because I was trusted to do the job. I was a good decoy, because potential bank robbers never expected a kid to be carrying the cash.

While working in the bank marketing department, I discovered my love for selling. One year I signed up over one hundred small businesses to join the chamber of commerce. Selling has been the foundation of my insurance career for over twenty years now. I get great satisfaction about talking with people regarding insurance services my company provides.

I graduated from college during an economic recession, so starting a sales job did not seem like the best opportunity. I became an auditor for a large CPA firm. Although I was not passionate about the work, this job gave me an extraordinary amount of business knowledge. I was often referred to as a bean counter, which is actually true. During one business audit of an automobile company, I counted over 10,000 batteries during an inventory audit.

As a newlywed husband with a new partner in my life, I needed to make more money. Beth and I became homeowners, so we had a mortgage to pay. We also had car payments and daily living expenses. I found a new job earning more money as a real estate property manager. I managed shopping centers throughout the Southeast. Most of the centers were in metro Atlanta, but six were located in cities along the Gulf Coast. Each month I drove to New Orleans, Louisiana; Pascagoula, Mississippi; Mobile, Alabama; Pensacola, Florida; Milton, Florida; and Fort Walton Beach, Florida. Each shopping center was anchored by a big retail store and a large grocery store with small local businesses. The leasing and management were easy. My biggest challenge was dealing with hurricanes every year. Damaging winds required constant repairs to our buildings.

One year, a local church decided to have a tent revival in the shopping center parking lot. Revivals are OK with me, but the church didn't ask for permission. The giant tent was erected in the middle of the parking lot, causing a parking problem for our shoppers. I arrived at the shopping center to meet with the church leaders. I told them about our safety and liability concerns with so many people and so many cars. Company management and the tenants requested that the tent be taken down and moved to another location. I was the messenger for this information, and one of the church ladies didn't take the news so well. She started chasing my coworker and hitting her with a Bible. She called me Mr. Bembries and threatened to contact the TV show called *The 700 Club*. Other church leaders calmed her down, and we all decided it was best to move the tent revival to a new location.

I worked two other part-time jobs to supplement my income for our growing family. One job was very rewarding, and the other was very difficult. I worked as a night school professor at the local community college. Working with the students was rewarding. But working all day and then lecturing the students until ten o'clock in the evening was exhausting. The most difficult job I ever performed was working as a headhunter or recruiter. I worked for weeks at trying to place people in jobs to find out they were not interested.

My dream of owning my own business finally came true. I began my insurance career as a financed community agent. Nationwide Insurance Company was my business partner. They started me in a three-year management training program with a business plan and income subsidies. I quickly learned that hard work and determination were the keys to success. I committed my work to God and used the skills and talents He gave me. I determined that success was based on goals and a process. Auto insurance, home insurance, and life insurance were the company products. I became an expert with knowledge about each product. I believe in the importance of insurance because I saw firsthand the devastation caused by hurricanes and storms. I was in a car accident and insurance replaced my totally damaged vehicle. When my father died, it was life insurance that allowed us to stay in our home.

The fear of losing my job was a big factor in keeping me motivated to work hard. Each month for three years, I was required to insure at least twenty-five items. That usually included ten autos, ten homes, and five lives. It was a challenging task because the servicing requirement became more demanding as I grew in size. Fortunately, I hired Tammy Totten who became my co-worker and helped me manage customers for over 20 years. With Tammy's help, my plan seemed easy. Just talk to people every day and build business relationships through your discussions. Talk to people, set appointments, write policies. Talk to people, set appointments, write policies. Talk to people, set appointments, write policies. That was all I needed to do to be successful.

There were three groups of people that I needed to talk with every day. The first included friends and family. The second was my referral group. This included business partners like mortgage brokers, real estate agents, and car salesmen. The final group I talked with every day was my current customers, cross-selling new products to existing customers.

Life insurance was sometimes challenging because the people who wanted life insurance did not meet the underwriting guidelines. I've always followed the business practice of meeting customers in their home. It was more helpful to me to complete the underwriting inspection and the customers felt more comfortable at home. Marijuana use is not legal in most states and will require life insurance to be declined. One evening I made a life insurance visit to a group of people who had been smoking marijuana all day. When I opened the front door, a puff of smoke exited the house. Everyone was high, and it was impossible to ask my underwriting questions. They all seemed hungry, and they just could not stop laughing at everything I asked. I politely told them that a life insurance plan would not work at the present time. As I left the home, they were the happiest people I met that day.

I had another call one day from a guy who wanted to buy twenty-five life insurance policies. This sounded too good to be true, and I was right. When I showed up for the appointment that night, he turned out to be a Gypsy. He wanted to buy twenty-five life insurance policies for his Gypsy friends who were traveling across country. I told him that it probably wouldn't work out because I needed to meet and interview the twenty-five people needing life insurance. He said that would be impossible, but if I ever needed my house painted or new asphalt on the driveway to give him a call. He then got in his pickup truck and drove away.

Another interesting event happened when a sweet, little lady called me for a life insurance policy. I drove to her home in downtown Atlanta to get the policy started. She answered all of my questions, and I was ready to complete the application to make a life insurance policy effective that day. I needed to give her a life insurance actuary chart that I left in my car that was parked on the street in front of her apartment. When I walked down the steps to my car, I noticed two ladies leaning against my car. It was during the evening and I quickly realized that these two ladies were ladies of the night. They asked me if I was interested in buying a good time, and it was not life insurance. Suddenly, my sweet, little customer ran out of the apartment building carrying her broom. She started swinging the broom at the two ladies and told them that no prostitute was going to proposition her life insurance agent! The streets were cleared, and I started the life insurance policy for my sweet friend that night.

In recent years, I have become an active farm insurance agent. I have thoroughly enjoyed traveling to rural communities in our state to become a trusted farm insurance agent. In my opinion, farming is the most important industry in our country. If we don't have farms, we don't have food. It's that simple. I have seen firsthand the trials and tribulations faced by farmers every day. Storms, disease, drought, and farm liability are some of the daily difficulties.

Recently, a beef cattle farm customer lost twelve cows that were struck by lightning. A tornado destroyed two chicken houses that were owned by another farm customer. The two houses were completely destroyed, and he lost 40,000 chickens. A row crop farm customer was harvesting his soybeans when the combine tractor he was driving caught on fire. The tractor was completely destroyed by the fire and there was extensive damage to the crop remaining in the field. The refrigeration system in a truck carrying milk from a dairy failed. Thousands of gallons of milk were spoiled and had to be dumped. A farmer was giving riding lessons at the horse farm. A student fell off a horse during the lesson and sued the farmer for medical injuries.

One of the most amazing stories happened to a customer who owns a restaurant. During severe storms that often occur in the spring, two tornadoes approached a small town. It was 2011 and the town was Joplin, Missouri. The massive storm lasted for thirty-eight minutes and the two tornadoes destroyed the entire town. There were 158 fatalities, and 1,100 people were injured. The winds destroyed and damaged over $2 billion in property. It was the costliest tornado in US history. The only building in town to survive this massive destruction was my customer's Waffle House restaurant. The restaurant was used to feed all of the rescue and recovery workers. It was a miracle from God, and the restaurant owner's name was Mr. Miracle.

Bill started a small business from scratch in the year 2000. Today Hembree Insurance has three offices and provides auto, home, farm, business and life insurance to many customers.

But Jesus said, "Let the children come to me. Don't stop them! For the kingdom of heaven belongs to those who were like these children."
—Matthew 19:14 (NLT)

Children, obey your parents in everything, for this pleases the Lord.
—Colossians 3:20 (NIV)

Train up a child in the way he should go; even when he is old, he will not depart from it.
—Proverbs 22:6 (ESV)

Children are a gift from the Lord, they are a reward from him.
—Psalm 127:3 (NLT)

I have no greater joy than this, to hear of my children walking in the truth.
—3 John 1:4 (NASB95)

Fathers, do not provoke your children to anger by the way you treat them. Rather, bring them up with the discipline and instruction that comes from the Lord.
—Ephesians 6:4 (NLT)

These commandments that I give you today are to be on your hearts. Impress them on your children. Talk about them when you sit at home and when you walk along the road, when you lie down and when you get up.
—Deuteronomy 6:6–7 (NIV)

All your children will be taught by the Lord, and great will be their peace.
—Isaiah 54:13 (NIV)

Children, obey your parents because you belong to the Lord, for this is the right thing to do. Honor your father and mother. This is the first commandment with a promise: if you honor your father and mother, Things will go well for you, and you will have a long life on the earth.
—Ephesians 6:1–3 (NLT)

Children's children are a crown to the aged, and parents are the pride of their children.
—Proverbs 17:6 (NIV)

Discipline your children, and they will give you peace of mind and will make your heart glad.
—Proverbs 29:17 (NLT)

My four greatest accomplishments in life are my wife, Beth, and my three sons, Will, Thomas, and Miles. My wife and children are truly a gift from God. Fatherhood is a great reward. Raising your children in the ways of God is the foundation of a healthy family. Discipline, guidance, counseling, and encouragement are necessary to help children grow into responsible adults. Teaching good character traits to a child will help them tremendously as they grow into adulthood. The influence of a father figure in the home will help a young man become a good husband and a good parent. Parenting can be difficult, but it is much easier when the responsibilities are shared by the mother and father. Each parent plays a unique and important role in the daily development of their children.

In 1995 William Aubrey Hembree Jr. was born. He brought so much joy and happiness to Beth and me. We surrounded Will with love. In 2000, the family grew with a wonderful surprise. Twins! Thomas Andrew Hembree and Miles Alexander Hembree were born. These three boys became the center of our world. Helping them grow and learn was our full commitment. School, sports, music, and much more made parenting the greatest job on earth.

Will was born on Friday, April 21, 1995. The time was 9:20 p.m. and we welcomed our firstborn child into this world. Thomas and Miles were born on Saturday, October 21, 2000. The time was 11:22 and 11:23 p.m. We welcomed our twins into this world.

Will is a natural leader and a great manager of people. He is very intelligent and has great analytical skills. Will has a wonderful sense of humor. He is honest. He is a great communicator and commands attention. He is responsible and gets things done. He is a goal setter and displays the highest level of confidence.

Thomas is a leader who is focused on accomplishments. He is loyal to his friends and followers. Thomas is athletic and focused on physical and mental success. He is passionate about his pursuits in life. He is attentive to those around him. He is intelligent. He is organized and focused on details. He is honest. He is a perfectionist and very disciplined in his work.

Miles is a leader who is outgoing and has an internal driving force to succeed. He is dependable and gets the job done. He is a hard worker and a great provider. He is a free spirit and loves the outdoors. He is honest. He is kind, generous, and helpful to others. He is intelligent with an engineering mind. Miles has a very positive attitude.

William is a classic English name. It means resolute protector or strong-willed warrior. Will carries my name, and my hope is that my boys will have children and continue the Hembree family name.

Thomas comes from the Hebrew word meaning twin. Thomas was born one minute before Miles. St. Thomas was a twin and also one of the twelve disciples of Jesus Christ. Thomas is also a family name on Beth's mother's side.

Miles comes from the Latin word for soldier. Miles was also named for the ancient warrior Alexander the Great, who was a king, commander, and statesman. Miles is also a family name on Beth's mother's side.

When I read the Bible, I am intrigued by the remarkable characters and their resolute personalities. Will reminds me of King David. Thomas reminds me of the prophet Moses. Miles reminds me of the apostle Peter.

The Bible calls David a man after God's own heart. Like David, Will is compassionate, loving, kind, and merciful. David was a great leader and managed to bring the twelve tribes of Israel together. David was a hero because he followed commands without a doubt and sacrificed himself for the good of others. David had his weaknesses, but his heart was close to God. David was a humble shepherd, yet he was confident and sure of himself and dismissed the opinion of others. His humility became clear early in his youth when he killed the giant Goliath with a sling stone, refusing the opportunity to wear the king's royal armor.

Moses is one of the most important prophets in the Bible. Like Moses, Thomas is a great leader. They are both charismatic and filled with wisdom, patience, empathy, and humility. Moses was well educated and trained by the Egyptian pharaoh. Moses received the Ten Commandments directly from God to share with his people. Moses led the Israelites out of Egypt and into the Promised Land of Canaan. Moses was an author and hero in the Bible. Moses met face-to-face with God and is called the lawgiver. His greatest gift was his personal relationship with God. Moses obeyed God's orders, and God performed amazing miracles through him against great danger from Pharaoh and overwhelming challenges.

Peter was one of the twelve apostles of Jesus Christ. Like Peter, Miles is a man of absolute faith. They are both fishermen and men of great physical strength. Jesus told Peter to follow Him and He would make him a fisher of men. Jesus gave Peter the keys to the kingdom of heaven. Peter proclaimed that Jesus was the Son of the Living God. Jesus called Peter the foundation of the church. Jesus said you are Peter, and on this rock, I will build my church. Peter walked on water with Jesus and healed the crippled. Peter was one of Jesus's closest friends and the leader of His twelve disciples. In John 21:15–17 (ESV), Jesus directed Peter to care for His church. Three times, Jesus commanded Peter to take care of His Christian followers. Jesus said, Peter feed my lambs, tend my sheep, feed my sheep. Peter preached the good news of salvation through Jesus Christ.

Will Hembree

Will Hembree

Thomas Hembree

Thomas Hembree

Miles Hembree

Miles Hembree

Family vacation trip to St. Simons Island, Georgia.

Brotherly love with Thomas, Will and Miles. Precious little boys.

Being a dad is the best job ever. Miles, Thomas, Will and Bill.

Children are a gift from God. Miles, Thomas and Will.

Playing in the creek made growing up in the country fun. Miles, Will and Thomas.

When Beth and I had our children, we were overwhelmed with this new responsibility. Family and friends were so helpful to assist us in our new parenting role. Just when you think everything is under control and the job seems easy, complications and trouble can develop. Two remarkable women always appeared to save our day and help us overcome disasters. We were blessed with grandmothers. Charlotte Rainwater and Monta Raye Hembree rescued us on many occasions.

These ladies had the experience we needed to help us be good parents. It is so important to include grandparents in the lives of your children. The grandparents' love is a special love that is unique and needed by every child. Always accept help from a grandmother when it is offered. Raising children can be challenging. Charlotte and Monta Raye were always special role models for our boys. They never missed a birthday or holiday to spend time with the boys. They never missed a school play or music recital. They never missed a baseball game or sporting event. They were the best cheerleaders for the boys and encouraged them to do their best. If the boys were sick, they helped to nurse them back to good health. Their old-fashioned remedies were usually all that was needed. For babysitting, doctors' visits, and those rare emergencies, a grandmother was always available to help us. They never said no, and they never complained when we asked for help. We were so grateful to have them near our home. They guided our boys with an example of kindness and directed them to love one another.

Charlotte is always so excited to see her grandsons. She was always the first to arrive on Christmas morning so she could experience the childhood joy and excitement of Christmas. When the babies were newborns, she would stay overnight in the guestroom. She was up every hour to feed the babies so Beth could get some much-needed rest. She loved to take the babies on stroller rides through the neighborhood. She is a wonderful cook and prepared many meals for us all to enjoy. She read books to the boys and told them stories about her family. She was so excited when the boys were old enough to spend the night at her home. She gave them ice cream, and they watched the Atlanta Braves play baseball. It was OK to spoil them because that's what grandmothers do. Charlotte made sure the boys were safe and happy with plenty of things to do. Charlotte especially loved taking the boys to her church on Sunday morning. She was so proud of them and showed them off to the ladies in her Sunday school class. She played a major role in the growth and development of our children. Charlotte is a wonderful grandmother, and she gave our sons a unique and loving relationship that no one can ever replace. She will always be my sons Bobo, and the memories they share will last forever.

Monta Raye raised five children on her own as a single mother after the sudden death of my father. She knew firsthand about the daily difficulties and struggles new parents face. She knew that raising a child was a twenty-four hour a day job, seven days a week. Hard work was never a challenge for her because she knew what had to be done to survive. Beth and I worked so she was the daily caregiver for Will over several years. Playtime and naptime were always the two greatest priorities. When Beth became pregnant with the twins, we decided the best job for her and our children was to be a stay-at-home mom. Monta Raye continued to help us whenever we called. She was also a very engaged grandmother. She attended every event that was planned for our sons at school and in sports. She traveled with us on business trips, watching the boys while we were away at meetings. She was filled with life and energy. Birthdays and holidays were her favorite celebrations, and she encouraged the boys to enjoy life. She taught our children so many life lessons that related to her many experiences. She always said that your family should be a reflection of who you are and the family that prays together, stays together. She gave our family so many precious memories. We will always cherish the love and devotion she gave to our sons. She was a wonderful grandmother, and her boys called her Mae Mae.

As Beth and I have moved through the stages in life, we look forward to the day when we can become a grandmother and grandfather. We have been blessed with two extraordinary women to learn from. They both set the greatest examples for us to follow. We look forward to that joyous day when our grandchildren call us Papa and BeBe.

Charlotte Mozley Rainwater and her grandchildren, Thomas, Miles and Will.

Monta Raye Hembree and her grandson Will.

MY PILGRIM'S JOURNEY TO THE HOLY LAND

Life is a journey, and I feel it is important to engage in activities that fulfill your interest. The Bible is the Word of God, and reading it will enhance your life. Reading biblical text and stories help us follow a path of righteous living. When we use our imagination, the Bible stories come alive and we imagine the events as they happened. If you are a Christian and your faith leads you, I encourage you to make a trip to the Holy Land in Israel.

I have read the Bible from start to finish several times, and I try to start my day with spiritual devotions and prayer. Reading scripture in the morning gives me peace of mind and encouragement for the day ahead. I never wanted to watch life pass by sitting in my home. Reading the Bible was not enough for me. I wanted to walk where Jesus walked. I wanted to walk through Jerusalem and visit the stable in Bethlehem. I wanted to feel the waters of the Jordan River and worship Jesus on the Mount of Olives. I was compelled by the Holy Spirit to make a Christian pilgrim's journey to Israel. During the Easter month of April in the year 2000, I set out on a life-changing trip. Two thousand years earlier, my Lord and Savior, Jesus Christ, walked on this earth as a man and saved me from my sins. He bore the sins and transgressions of an evil world with his blood and death. After three days, He arose from the dead and ascended into heaven to sit at the right hand of God. He performed miracles and preached the good news of eternal life in heaven for those of us who believe that He is the Son of God and the Savior of the world.

While I was in the Holy Land, I experienced unforgettable visions that lifted my soul. I was baptized in the church when I was sixteen years old. Jesus was baptized in the Jordan River, and as I stood on the banks of this remarkable river, I was overwhelmed by the Holy Spirit. I had to touch and feel the cool water that Jesus felt. I needed to be baptized again and remember that Jesus washed away my sins. I needed to cleanse my mind and soul through Jesus in the water of the Jordan River. As the preacher laid me under the water and baptized me in the name of the Father, the Son, and the Holy Spirit, I opened my eyes. I was immersed under the waters of the Jordan River. It seemed as though time had stopped as I held my breath under the cool water. I could see the light of the world underwater. The water was crystal clear, and the sun delivered its rays through the water. The sun was shining so brightly directly above me. It was the greatest light I had ever seen. The Holy Spirit filled my body and reminded me that Jesus is the light of the world. The preacher raised me up out of the water, and joy filled my heart. My faith was rewarded by a sign from God. I live by faith and not by sight. But with this experience, I was touched by the Son of God, Jesus Christ.

Jesus began His ministry and performed great miracles in the area around the Sea of Galilee. Our travel group was staying in a hotel in the town of Tiberias along the seashore. The Sea of Galilee is actually a large freshwater lake surrounded by small fishing villages. One night, I couldn't sleep. Sometime around midnight, I left my hotel room and walked to the shore of the Sea of Galilee. I sat down on a large rock, staring at the water, and began to pray. There was no moon that night, and darkness covered the land. Security lights at the hotel were shining bright and cast light over the water. Once again, the Holy Spirit came upon me and I opened my eyes. In the distance over the lake, I saw a snow-white dove flying above the water. The Holy Spirit reminded me that the Spirit of God descended onto Jesus in the form of a dove after His baptism. Midnight and darkness were all around me. But this white dove flying in the darkness lifted my spirit and gave me peace in my heart. I live by faith, not by sight. But I believe this white dove was a symbol of peace for me from God.

Capernaum was a fishing village along the North Shore of the Sea of Galilee. Jesus performed many miracles in Capernaum. It was the center of His public ministry. Jesus cured Peter's mother-in-law from her sickness. Christ also cured the paralyzed man who was lowered to Him through the roof. He performed an exorcism at the synagogue. Jesus healed the royal official's son in Capernaum.

Tabgha is another area along the Sea of Galilee. This is the location where Jesus fed five thousand followers. He multiplied five loaves of bread and two fish into a miracle that fed thousands of people. After His resurrection, Jesus appeared to His disciples here on the seashore.

The Mount of Beatitudes is a hill along the shore of the Sea of Galilee. This is where Jesus delivered the Sermon on the Mount. Jesus said the following:

> Blessed are the poor in spirit: for theirs is the kingdom of heaven. Blessed are they that mourn: for they shall be comforted. Blessed are the meek: for they shall inherit the earth. Blessed are they which do hunger and thirst after righteousness: for they shall be filled. Blessed are the merciful: for they shall obtain mercy. Blessed are the pure in heart: for they shall see God. Blessed are the peacemakers: for they shall be called the children of God. Blessed are they which are persecuted for righteousness' sake: for theirs is the kingdom of heaven.

Cana is a village in Galilee where Jesus attended a wedding ceremony. He performed another great miracle when He turned water into wine for the marriage celebration. In another nearby village, called Bethsaida, Jesus healed a blind man.

Mount Tabor is another significant area in Galilee. The Transfiguration of Jesus Christ occurred here. The disciples watched as Jesus began to radiate light as He had a conversation with Moses and Elijah.

Mount Carmel is also located in this area. In the Bible, the prophet Elijah defeated the false priest of Baal on this mountain. Elijah proved that there is only one true God.

Just a short distance away is the town of Nazareth. This is the boyhood home of Jesus and the place He worked as a carpenter. During His ministry, Jesus preached in the synagogue at Nazareth. But His message was rejected by the people of this town.

The Bible tells us the story of Mary and Joseph in their journey from Nazareth to Bethlehem. The actual distance between these two towns is just over seventy miles. The young couple traveled to Bethlehem for the most important event that ever happened: the birth of Jesus Christ. Our travel group visited the Church of the Nativity. This church was built above the stable where Jesus was born over two thousand years ago. After you enter the church, there is a passageway that descends into a cave or grotto. The manger scene is a holy place and is marked by an inlaid silver star. "Oh little town of Bethlehem, how still we see the lie, above thy deep and dreamless sleep, the silent stars go by." Our group sang many wonderful Christmas carols as we stood in the sacred place.

South of Bethlehem are the ruins of the city called Jericho. Joshua and the Israelites carried the Ark of the Covenant, which contained the Ten Commandments, around Jericho. For seven days, they walked around the city, and on the seventh day, they sounded the ram's horns and gave a mighty shout. The walls of Jericho came tumbling down, and God gave the city to Joshua and the Israelites.

Nearby you will find the Jewish fortress of Masada and the Dead Sea. Masada was built by King Herod. Jewish patriots made their last stand against the Roman army here seventy-three years after the death and resurrection of Jesus. The Dead Sea Scrolls were also found in this area and give significant historical records about the time of Jesus. The Dead Sea is so thick with salt that your body floats on the surface.

Jerusalem, and the area around the city, is the most significant place in the Bible. Jesus, the Messiah, was crucified, died, and was buried in Jerusalem. After three days, Jesus arose from the dead in this city, and He ascended into heaven. The Church of the Holy Sepulcher is the location where Jesus was crucified on the cross. Nearby is an empty tomb called the Garden Tomb. The tomb is empty because Jesus arose from the dead—on Easter Sunday.

There are so many significant Christian sites in Jerusalem. The Via Dolorosa Street marks the path and stages that Jesus walked as He carried the cross to save us from our sins. Just outside the city gates are the Garden of Gethsemane and the Mount of Olives. Two-thousand-year-old trees are still living in the place where Jesus prayed and wept before He was arrested in the Garden of Gethsemane. The Mount of Olives is the sacred place where Jesus ascended into heaven to sit at the right hand of God.

Inside the old city of Jerusalem, you will find the upper room. This is the location where Jesus and His twelve disciples shared the Last Supper. At the supper, Jesus blessed the bread and broke it, telling the disciples, "Take, eat; this is my body." Then Jesus passed a cup of wine to them, saying, "Drink from it, this is my blood, which is poured out for many for the forgiveness of sins. Do this in remembrance of me."

Nearby in the old city is the Temple Mount. This is the location of the temple built by King Solomon. In the Old Testament of the Bible, the temple was a sacred place where heaven and Earth were united. The temple was a symbol of God's desire to live among His people and rule the world through them. Today, the Western Wall of the old temple is still used. It is where Jews can pray.

When I was in the city of Jerusalem, I felt compelled to pray at the Western Wall. Daily prayer is very significant to me. I needed to pray in this holy place. It is a common ritual to leave written daily prayers between the rocks of the Western Wall. The ancient wall is massive and the area is busy with people. I carefully drafted three written prayers on small pieces of paper that I could leave at the wall. The whole experience was overwhelming as I walked forward with my prayers. Suddenly, behind me, security guards were yelling at me to stop. I was so nervous. What did I do wrong? I was afraid. Somehow, they knew I was a Gentile, a Christian. This was a Jewish site. They surrounded me and said, "Sir, you are praying in the wrong section. You are praying with the women; all men pray down there on that end." Well, I was very embarrassed but relieved that I had not broken any rules. I walked to the men's section of the wall and left my written prayers, inserting them between the rocks.

Our last stop in the Holy Land was at the ancient Roman city of Caesarea on the Mediterranean Sea. The ancient Roman amphitheater still exists today. I was honored by my travel group to read the Bible before them in this amphitheater. The acoustics are perfect, and my voice carried around the amphitheater. I read Acts 23. I told the story about the apostle Paul who was arrested without charges for being a Christian. He spent two years under house arrest in Caesarea before he was sent to Rome.

Bill visits the ancient town of Capharnaum or Capernaum on the Sea of Galilee in Israel. Jesus performed many miracles here and chose his disciples Peter, Andrew, and Matthew from this fishing town.

Bill is baptized in the Jordan River during the Easter month of April 2000. The Jordan River holds a special place in Christian tradition, for it is here that Christ was baptized by his cousin, John the Baptist. Matthew 3:13-17 (NIV)

Bill visited the town of Bethlehem where Jesus was born. The silver star shows the manger area where baby Jesus laid in the stable with Mary and Joseph on Christmas Eve.

Bill visits the garden of Gethsemane outside Jerusalem. Jesus prayed here and was overwhelmed with anguish and sorrow. He was betrayed and arrested here before his crucifixion. These olive trees are over 2500 years old and living when Jesus walked on the earth.

The empty tomb in Jerusalem where Jesus was buried for three days until His resurrection on Easter Sunday.

Inside the empty tomb where Jesus was buried for three days before His resurrection and ascension to Heaven to sit at the Right Hand of God.

Golgotha also called Calvary is the skull-shaped hill outside Jerusalem where Jesus was crucified to save us from our sins. John 19:17 (NIV)

Bill read God's word in the ancient Roman amphitheater in Caesarea Israel. Paul the Apostle was kept prisoner for two years in Caesarea. Paul baptized the Roman centurion Cornelius here who was the first gentile to convert to Christianity.

The Eastern gate of Jerusalem is where Jesus entered the city on Palm Sunday.
When Jesus returns, he will travel through the Eastern gate.

THE GRAND CANYON: GOD'S MASTERPIECE

If you want to see a masterpiece created by God, visit the Grand Canyon in the state of Arizona. When you walk to the edge of the Grand Canyon, you will experience one of the most spectacular views in the world. Words cannot describe this awesome view. It is truly a God-given piece of artwork. As the sun moves across the sky toward sunset, the colors of the canyon are constantly changing. There is a reflection on the rocks, and it is a beautiful sight. The mighty Colorado River looks like a tiny stream as it twists and turns at the bottom of the canyon. Thousands of feet below, the river cuts through the desert rock, creating quiet waters and raging rapids.

I highly recommend the Grand Canyon National Park trip. Once again, the Hembree family was on another summer adventure. The view from the top of the Grand Canyon was spectacular, but I wanted to go to the bottom and touch the waters of this amazing river. I contacted the National Park Service to discover ways to reach the bottom of the canyon. They had only two options available. The first was hiking along trails to the bottom. The second was riding a donkey along trails to the bottom. Neither of these two options seemed safe for my young family. The steep cliffs and narrow trails were just too dangerous. My research paid off. Most of the Grand Canyon is surrounded by an Indian reservation. I discovered that one of the tribes has a secret road that winds to the bottom of the canyon. We hired a Jeep with a driver who had special permission to use the road. I loaded up my family in the Jeep and we drove down to the Colorado River. We had a picnic lunch on a sandy beach, and the boys played in the calm water.

I wanted my family to experience the Grand Canyon in as many ways as possible. A rafting trip down the river seemed like a great adventure. The Glen Canyon Dam near Page, Arizona, is a great starting point. We all climbed aboard a large raft at the bottom of the dam and started our journey down the river. The red rock cliffs on both sides of the river climbed up to over one thousand feet high. We slowly floated along the river at the bottom of this massive canyon.

Several hours into the trip, we stopped on a small, sandy beach along the riverbank. In this area, we visited ancient Indian carvings of animals and people on the rocks. The boys swam in the ice-cold river, and we enjoyed our view looking up from the bottom of the canyon.

Our next adventure was looking down at the canyon high above the land. There are several companies available to take helicopter rides over and across the canyon. I strongly recommend taking a helicopter ride if you visit the Grand Canyon. Our family of five boarded the helicopter and set out above the tree line at a high rate of speed. We all wore headphones and were entertained by music from the movie *Chariots of Fire.* Suddenly the ground below us disappeared, and the deep canyon opened up all around us. This bird's-eye view from above was absolutely amazing. The enormous size and depth of the Grand Canyon is an amazing sight.

There are other sites to see in Arizona that I highly recommend being a part of your itinerary. In the northeast corner of Arizona is a place called Monument Valley Park. Monument Valley is the most photographed place in the world. Movies and advertisers have used this godly masterpiece for many years. Towering sandstone buttes rise up thousands of feet above the red sand desert. Wind and rain erosion have created some of the most interesting rock formations I have ever seen. Western movies starring John Wayne were filmed along the seventeen-mile valley. Driving along the Monument Valley Road will lead you to believe you were on the Planet Mars. The rocks and sand all around you are red. The Navajo Indian tribe has a nice museum I think you should visit while in the park. I also recommend visiting the Navajo Indian cliff dwellings. It was an enjoyable hike for my family to see these ancient villages carved on cliffs.

Another fascinating place to visit is called Meteor Crater. Fifty thousand years ago, a giant meteor from outer space crashed into the earth, leaving a giant hole. This site represents the best-preserved meteor impact site in the world. This enormous rock from space created a whole almost six hundred feet deep and over four thousand feet wide. My family enjoyed the windy walk along the edge of the giant crater. My boys enjoyed visiting the space museum also located at the site.

Two other nearby towns are worth visiting on your trip. If you are a fan of the Eagles, a legendary rock 'n' roll band from the 1970s, you must stop in Winslow, Arizona. Standing on the corner in Winslow are lyrics from the song "Take It Easy." Historic Route 66 runs to the town. Flagstaff, Arizona, is another western town you will want to visit.

Sedona, Arizona, is another breathtaking desert town. We took a Jeep tour over the majestic red rock scenery across the desert. We needed the four-wheel-drive Jeep to climb up and down the red rock hills. The day was over one hundred degrees Fahrenheit so we stopped at the Red Rock River for a swim. The boys had a great time cooling off and playing in the rapids along the small river.

Be sure and plan a trip to Arizona so you can see all of these wonderful sites.

The Hembree family vacation trip to the Grand Canyon.

The Grand Canyon is beautiful. The rock colors are spectacular as the sun moves across the sky.

The Hembree family visits Monument Valley in Arizona. Over 100 movies and TV shows were filmed in the valley.

WESTERN BEAUTY

God's creations are all around us. He surrounds us with beauty for our eyes to behold. We need to open our eyes and embrace all of His creations. We need to escape the darkness of a closed world and renew our spirits in the nature around us that God created. There are several national parks in the western United States that should inspire us all to visit them. They are peaceful and serene places that display the awesome power of God's beauty.

Yosemite National Park is one of those places that will inspire you with its beauty. The giant granite mountains are mostly treeless and tower high in the sky above the valleys. The gray, granite mountains are a sharp contrast and color to the blue sky above and the green grassy meadows below. Heavy snow during the winter creates the most beautiful waterfalls I have ever seen. As the snow melts, the water pours off the granite peaks and falls over two thousand feet. El Capitan and Half Dome are the two largest rock formations and glow like fire at sunset. The mountains are so big that rock climbers sleep overnight anchored to the mountainside before reaching the summit the next day.

I had signed my family up for a park tour. We arrived at the ranger station late and the open tour bus was leaving the parking lot. It was my fault for being late so I didn't want to cause a commotion and stop the tour bus. I told Beth and the boys to roll their windows down and we followed the tour bus around the park. We heard every detail the park ranger spoke about and learned many interesting facts about Yosemite. When the tour was over, we walked around the beautiful meadows and took some great pictures of the waterfalls.

There are two other amazing national parks that you should see, and they are all about trees. Redwood National Park and Sequoia National Park contain the biggest trees in the world. Some redwood trees live for over two thousand years. The redwoods are also the tallest trees in the world and climb to almost four hundred feet high above the forest floor. As my family walked along the forest trails among the towering redwoods, we recognized the awesome power of God's creation. The sequoia trees are different. They are tall but very wide around the trunk. The boys wanted to see the General Sherman, which is the world's largest tree. This sequoia tree is over thirty-six feet wide and 275 feet tall. The boys were tiny as they climbed around and inside these giant trees. These trees are the largest and oldest living creations on earth. They are wonderful to see.

Death Valley National Park is the hottest, driest, and lowest park in the United States. It is truly a place you must see and experience the most extreme conditions anywhere in the world. In this valley, the record temperature is 134 degrees Fahrenheit. Death Valley is the hottest place on earth. As I drove the family in our rented minivan, we descended into this hot and desolate place that felt like a real furnace. The dry heat was 115 degrees Fahrenheit during our summer visit. We stayed at the Furnace Creek Inn that had a great air conditioning system. It was over one hundred degrees Fahrenheit outside during the night. The valley gets only one inch of rain each year. The hotel swimming pool felt like a hot tub. Even with these extreme conditions, there is so much beauty in the desert and mountains surrounding Death Valley.

One of the most beautiful driving experiences in the country is along the Pacific Coast Highway. Big Sur Park gives you stunning views of the bright-blue waters of the Pacific Ocean. Sand Dollar Beach is a sandy beach and great for walking and exploring this area. We saw large groups of sea lions basking in the sun along the shore. Powerful waves crash against the rocks, and the water is colored in many shades of blue. We visited the Hearst Castle, Pebble Beach Golf Course, and the towns of Carmel and Monterey.

As we continued seeing the beautiful sites along the Pacific Coast Highway, we arrived at the Golden Gate Bridge National Park. The Golden Gate Bridge is an iconic American symbol. It is a beautiful engineering masterpiece. We wanted to get the full experience of seeing this bridge, so we parked the minivan and walked across it. The slow walk enabled us to soak up our surroundings. The views were spectacular.

The Hembree family visit Yosemite National Park in California.

The Hembree family visit Death Valley National Park where the temperature was hot at 115 degrees Fahrenheit.

At Sequoia National Park Thomas and Miles stand in front of a sequoia tree that is 36 feet wide and 275 feet tall.

Big Sur Park along the Pacific Coast Highway in California.

We decided to walk across the Golden Gate Bridge to enjoy the spectacular view.

We the people of the United States, in order to form a more perfect union, establish justice, ensure domestic tranquility, provide for the common defense, promote the general welfare, and secure the blessings of liberty to ourselves and our posterity, do ordain and establish this Constitution for the United States of America.
—Preamble to the United States Constitution, 1787

We hold these truths to be self-evident, that all men are created equal, that they are endowed by their Creator with certain unalienable rights, that among these are life, liberty, and the pursuit of happiness.
—The Declaration of Independence, Thomas Jefferson, 1776

I pledge allegiance to the flag of the United States of America, and to the Republic, for which it stands, one nation, under God, indivisible, with liberty and justice for all.
—The Pledge of Allegiance, 1954

In God We Trust. [This means the political and economic prosperity of the nation is in God's hands.]
—The official motto of the United States, 1956

It is the duty of all nations, to acknowledge the providence of Almighty God, to obey his will, to be grateful for his benefits, and humbly to implore his protection and favor.
—George Washington, president of the United States, 1789

I believe the Bible is the best gift God has ever given to man. All the good of the Savior of the world is communicated to us through the book.
—Abraham Lincoln, president of the United States, 1862

Without God, there is no virtue because there is no prompting of the conscience. Without God, we're mired in the material, that flat world that tells us only what the senses perceive. Without God, there is a coarsening of the society. And without God, democracy will not and cannot long endure. If we ever forget that we're one nation under God, then we will be a nation gone under.
Ronald Reagan, president of the United States, 1984

I believe the United States is the greatest nation in human history because we were founded on Judeo-Christian principles. We are one nation under God. I have always encouraged my family to be patriotic. To love their country and have respect and reverence for the government. To live as responsible citizens and obey the laws of the land. Freedom is our country's greatest gift.

I encourage everyone who reads this book to visit Washington, DC, our nation's capital. It is important to read about the foundation of our country, but it is equally important to personally visit the institutions of government that govern our lives daily.

Visit the White House, the people's house. The president and the executive branch of government are responsible for implementing and enforcing the laws written by Congress. The president is the highest representative of our country, commander-in-chief of the armed forces, and leader of the free world.

It is important to contact your senator or congressman to secure tickets for entry to the White House before you visit Washington. The visit is free and you and your family can walk through the historic halls and rooms of this magnificent home.

It is very important to know who your elected representatives are and to visit them during their work in Washington. The United States Capitol is the meeting place of the United States Congress and the seat of the legislative branch of the federal government. A capitol tour will give you and your family a glimpse of government at work. Legislation is debated on the floor of the Senate and the House of Representatives. Ideas are turned into bills, and bills are debated by members of Congress. If the idea is good and the majority of the members support the bill or resolution, it may become law if signed by the president. It is important to follow the news about events at the Capitol because a new law can have a great impact on your daily life. My family met our congressman. We visited his office across the street from the Capitol. He arranged for some great family pictures with the Capitol in the background.

The US Supreme Court represents our judicial branch of government. Its justices settle disputes and make the final determination on laws passed by Congress. They interpret the Constitution, ensuring the American people the promise of equal justice under law. A tour of the Supreme Court building will give you a firsthand view of our nation's most important courtroom.

A trip to Washington, DC, is a virtual history lesson. The Smithsonian Institute Museum will provide you with hours of interesting information and fascinating displays. My family had two favorite museums that we visited. The National Museum of Natural History was great. With dinosaur exhibits, animal exhibits and rock exhibits, the museum is truly a celebration of the natural world. Our other favorite was the National Museum of American History. Here we saw "The Star-Spangled Banner," George Washington's uniform, Abraham Lincoln's top hat, and Dorothy's ruby slippers from *The Wizard of Oz*. There was so much more to see, and all of these museums are free to visit.

Be sure to wear your walking shoes because you will want to visit all the monuments outside. The Washington Monument, the Lincoln Memorial, the Jefferson Memorial, and the war memorials are requirements to see as you walk around the national mall. Don't forget to visit the National Archives Museum, where you will see the original Declaration of Independence, the original Constitution, and the original Bill of Rights. They are all on display, and you must take time to see these historic documents.

During the summer vacation, my family visited another very important historical site for the United States. We rented a car in Washington, DC, and drove to Philadelphia, Pennsylvania. The drive was easy, and it turned out to be a great day trip. Every American should try to visit Independence Hall. This building in Philadelphia is the foundation of our country. It is the birthplace of the United States. A few God-fearing men decided freedom and liberty were worth dying for and living for their future. Tyranny, oppressive taxation, and the Boston massacre drove the colonist in America to declare their independence from the British government.

In 1776, the Declaration of Independence was signed in Independence Hall. Eleven years later in the same building, the United States Constitution was adopted at the Constitutional Convention. George Washington, Thomas Jefferson, and Benjamin Franklin were a few of the notable and courageous men who gathered in this historic hall. You will be surprised how small the room is where these historical events took place. Delegates from each colony joined together and shared their ideas during the hot summer days over two hundred years ago. God developed and inspired their minds with wisdom and profound knowledge to form one nation under God. Their faith in God and desire for freedom and liberty helped them to create what has become the most powerful, prosperous, and generous nation in human history.

We have celebrations on the Fourth of July each year because of the magnificent work and dedication done by those men in Independence Hall on July 4, 1776. The Liberty Bell is displayed nearby. It was used at Independence Hall and is a well-known symbol of freedom in the United States.

To continue your journey on understanding the greatness of our country, I highly recommend a summer family trip to Boston, Massachusetts. Boston was the staging ground that started the American Revolution. The colonists in Boston protested the high taxation and tyranny of the British government. The Boston massacre and the Boston Tea Party were pivotal events that started the Revolutionary War. Militiamen in the nearby towns of Lexington and Concord were the first to fight the British Army.

I recommend that you walk along Boston's iconic 2.5-mile Freedom Trail that connects sixteen historic sites. Local guides will give you historical facts and point out historical locations that make the walk a memorable event. You can visit Paul Revere's home and the Old North Church. You can visit Faneuil Hall, which hosted America's first town hall meetings by the colonists. Along this walk are so many fascinating places that changed the course of history. The walk was easy for my family, and we all loved the detailed stories of revolutionary life told by the guides.

"Give me your tired, your poor, your huddled masses yearning to breathe free, the wretched refuse of your teeming shore." These are the words of Emma Lazarus that are inscribed on a tablet at the base of the Statue of Liberty. The Statue of Liberty is an iconic symbol of American freedom. You must visit this impressive statue on a summer trip to New York City. The statue sits in New York Harbor and is a beacon of hope and freedom. It stands as the gateway to the United States. It stands in front of New York, the largest city in the United States. The Statue of Liberty and Ellis Island are important sites to visit to understand why we are one nation under God.

On September 11, 2001, the United States was changed forever. Our freedom and liberty were attacked by foreign terrorists. Islamic terrorists hijacked airplanes and two of the planes crashed into the twin towers of the World Trade Center in New York City, a third plane hit the Pentagon in Arlington, Virginia and the fourth plane crashed in a field in Shanksville, Pennsylvania. 2,977 people were killed by these attacks. This was the largest loss of life resulting from a foreign attack on American soil. A visit to the 9/11 Memorial and Museum in New York City will change your life forever. You will experience every human emotion during your encounter at this remarkable place.

Hembree summer family vacation trip to Washington, D.C.

The Hembree family in front of George Washington's home in Mount Vernon, Virginia

The Lincoln Memorial in Washington, D.C.

AMERICA: GOD'S WORK

O beautiful for spacious skies, for amber waves of grain, for purple mountain
majesties, above the fruited plain! America! America! God shed his grace on
thee and crown thy good with brotherhood from sea to shining sea!
O beautiful for pilgrim feet, whose stern, impassioned stress a thoroughfare
for freedom beat across the wilderness! America! America! God mend thine
every flaw, confirm thy soul in self-control, Thy liberty in law!
O beautiful for heroes proved in liberating strife, who more than self their
country loved, and mercy more than life! America! America! May God thy
gold refines till all success be nobleness and every gain divine!
O beautiful for patriot dream that sees beyond the years thine alabaster cities
gleam undimmed by human tears! America! America! God shed his grace on
thee and crown thy good with brotherhood from sea to shining sea!
—"America the Beautiful," Katharine Lee Bates

I have always believed that the United States of America is the most beautiful country in the world. I also believe that the United States of America is the greatest country ever created in human history. I always told my sons that before we venture out and see the world, we must first explore our own country. I have traveled to forty-one states and hope to visit all fifty.

Family time is the most important time in my opinion. Planning the summer vacation for my family allowed me to find new and exciting places for everyone to see. Each year I picked a destination. Then I would spend months researching places to stay and things to do. I became our family travel agent and put together some spectacular trips. We had wonderful trips to the beach and to the mountains, but I became fascinated with America's national parks.

I've always loved wildlife shows on television. When I was a kid, I was a wildlife nerd. Every Tuesday night at 7:30 p.m., I watched *Mutual of Omaha's Wild Kingdom* with Marlin Perkins. Seeing all those amazing animals on my television set fascinated me. I always dreamed that one day I would see the wildlife in person at Yellowstone National Park.

I told Beth and the boys that we should visit as many national parks as we could. The boys were in elementary school and old enough to understand and appreciate this opportunity. The first national park in the United States was Yellowstone. President Theodore Roosevelt had visited this amazing land in Wyoming. It was so unique and beautiful that it must be protected and preserved for everyone to see. The first national park summer vacation for the Hembree family was Yellowstone.

The vacation was wonderful, and as an animal lover, the park had the greatest diversity of wildlife I had ever seen. The animals are wild and completely untamed, but because they are protected, they were mostly unafraid. Vast herds of buffalo spread out across the grassy plains of Yellowstone Park. It was an amazing sight to see these huge animals so closely. It captured my imagination of those early days in the old western United States when millions of buffalo would migrate across the Great Plains. If you want to see wild animals up close in their natural habitat, Yellowstone Park is the best place in our country.

We also saw great herds of elk. The bull elk displayed massive antlers and walked majestically along the hillside. Groups of mule deer were also common across the grassy plains. The grass is so rich with nutrients and so abundant that the buffalo, elk, and mule deer maintain large populations.

During our visit, we also saw two of North America's greatest predators: the grizzly bear and the wolf. From the protection of our minivan, for several hours we watched a mother grizzly bear and her two cubs forage for food in a Yellowstone valley. We were all a little frightened as this massive animal walked near our vehicle. The grizzly was unafraid and acted as though we were not there.

We had another amazing experience with a wolf pack. This time our family got out of the minivan and watched the wolves play together like our family dogs do. Our protection from these deadly wild animals was the Yellowstone River. The river was very wide and the wolf pack had their den on the other side of the river. Wolf puppies emerged in and out of the den and were so cute. There were several puppies and they acted like family pets. It was so enjoyable to watch the wolf family. Yellowstone is a giant animal park. As I have said before, it is the best place in the country to drive around and see wild animals.

Yellowstone Park is best known for its geysers. My boys said walking through the park was like being in a giant science project. Yellowstone is actually a supervolcano that could erupt at any time. The superhot volcano under the parks surface heats up the water to create magnificent geysers. Our family sat together quietly along with all the other park visitors and watched the geyser called Old Faithful erupt. At exactly the same time every day, Old Faithful spews boiling hot water hundreds of feet into the air. Walking around the park, Beth said she felt like she was on the moon or another planet. Much of the park's landscape is desolate because of the hot water and gases that destroy surrounding trees and grassland.

The boys couldn't believe there could be snow in July. But they could see snow on top of Mount Washburn in Yellowstone Park. The winter snowfall is so heavy that piles of snow remain in certain areas throughout the year. The boys wanted to touch the snow so we set out on an adventure to climb the mountain. For several hours, we hiked up the mountainside as the snowy ground got closer and closer. Mount Washburn is 10,219 feet tall. We finally made it, and the boys threw snowballs at each other in the middle of July.

On top of the mountain, we saw two more amazing creatures. Perched in a tree overlooking the valley was a beautiful American bald eagle. I had never seen an eagle in the wild. It was so majestic and graceful. It looked big and powerful. It is such a wonderful choice to be our national symbol. Running along the hillside away from us was a herd of bighorn sheep. The bighorn rams had massive horns as they grazed on grass in this high elevation. What a beautiful sight to see a bald eagle and bighorn sheep on a snowy hillside in America's first national park.

We left the snow behind and started the hike down the hill where we parked our minivan. Weather changes quickly in Yellowstone and dark clouds were moving toward us. Within minutes, the wind began to blow and the air temperature dropped drastically. Our slow hike became a fast run as we all raced down the mountain. The brisk wind turned into a torrential rainstorm in such a short period of time. This summer thunderstorm was upon us, and we were getting soaking wet with every step. There was no cover for protection so we just kept walking faster and faster. Suddenly, the lightning started striking the ground all around us. At this point, I was carrying one of the boys on my back and holding the hands of the other two. The lightning intensified and the rumbling thunder was loud and frightening. I prayed to God to protect us and guide us safely out of this storm. Soon the rain stopped and the thunder and lightning moved away. The clouds opened up and the sun was shining brightly around us. We were wet from head to toe, but most importantly, we were safe.

We loaded ourselves into the minivan and headed to our overnight accommodations. As the Hembree travel agent, I made all of the overnight plans. On this night, I had no idea what was ahead of us. When we arrived at the address for our stay, I looked at Beth and the boys' reaction. The look was priceless. I began laughing so hard that I couldn't stop. The sign said primitive accommodations. It was literally a one-room shelter with a small bathroom. We made it through the night, and it turned out to be another adventure. The US Park Service maintains all of the overnight accommodations in the park, and they are very limited. If you want to stay in nicer facilities, it is important that you make your reservations up to one year in advance of your visit.

Just a short drive south of Yellowstone is another spectacular national park. Grand Teton National Park has stunning scenery with its iconic rugged mountain range. Three sharp-tipped mountains joined together to create the Teton Range. The beautiful mountains rise up to almost 14,000 feet above the plain. Lakes, rivers, and grasslands provide the perfect animal habitat for moose, pronghorn antelope, elk, buffalo, and grizzly bears.

The town of Jackson Hole is a great place to stay overnight. There is a wide range of shops, hotels, and restaurants to explore in the old, rustic town. We bought some western artwork in one of the local shops and enjoyed the unique atmosphere of this small town. The National Elk Refuge is located just outside town. Hundreds of old elk antlers have been collected to create an arch in the town square. There are museums and western shows that offer a variety of entertainment.

Our family enjoyed two fun adventures while visiting this town. We first had a chuckwagon dinner. We loaded up in a horse-drawn covered wagon for a ride across the valley. We traveled back in time like the original homesteaders riding in a wagon. We arrived at a perfect location with a beautiful view, and the cowboys had prepared a steak dinner for everyone to enjoy. The food was delicious. After dinner the cowboys entertained us with songs and storytelling. The covered wagon cookout was a great time for all of us. The next day, we enjoyed a rafting trip down the Snake River. Much of the river was calm and the trip was relaxing, but we did enjoy a few rapids that made the trip exciting. Driving around the area will allow you the opportunity to see the most beautiful scenery and mountain views.

There are some other great summer vacations that I highly recommend because they reflect the beauty of America. Everyone needs to take a trip to see the Mississippi River. It has so many connections to our culture and history. Its massive size will overwhelm you when you see it for the first time. It is the third largest river in the world. The river flows through ten states. A scenic roadway was built along the Mississippi River that will give you three thousand miles of spectacular views. Some of America's greatest cities were built along the river. You can visit Minneapolis, Minnesota; St. Louis, Missouri; Memphis, Tennessee; and New Orleans, Louisiana. These river towns offer great sites, food, and entertainment for everyone to enjoy.

Niagara Falls in New York is a very impressive place to see. You will be overwhelmed and amazed at the amount of water flowing over the falls. It is truly unbelievable to see 150,000 gallons of water pass over the falls every second. It's a beautiful sight as the mist rises high into the sky. My family took an exciting boat ride up the river to the bottom of the waterfall. The falling water is so powerful that we felt as though we were in a rainstorm. We had to wear rainsuits to stay partially dry. We also explored the underground tunnels behind the falls. Again, we experienced the mighty force of the falling water up close. During the evening, we enjoyed a spectacular light show that displayed beautiful colors against Niagara Falls.

Your family will never forget a summer vacation to the Florida Keys. It is a tropical paradise. My family took an unforgettable snorkeling trip at John Pennekamp Coral Reef State Park near Key Largo. A statue of Jesus stands in the middle of the coral reef. We saw many types of fish and coral formations. We followed a guide as we swam around these beautiful waters. You must enjoy deep sea fishing during a trip to the Keys and Islamorada is the fishing capital. The Gulf Stream flows just a few miles offshore so you will experience some of the best saltwater fishing in the world. On Marathon Key, I encourage you to visit the sea turtle rescue center. This turtle hospital rescues injured sea turtles. The sea turtles are rehabilitated and released back into the ocean. Bahia Honda State Park on Big Pine Key is another great place to swim in the clear water. Key West is a lively town and the southernmost point in the United States. Mallory Square is a great place where everyone in town watches the sunset. A boat ride to the Dry Tortugas is another great day trip adventure. You will never forget your drive along the seven-mile bridge crossing the ocean. The Florida Keys are an American treasure.

> Take me out to the ballgame, take me out with the crowd; buy me some peanuts and Cracker Jacks, I don't care if I never get back. For it's root, root, root for the home team, if they don't win, it's a shame. For it's one, two, three strikes, you're out, at the old ballgame.

Baseball is the All-American game. It is our national pastime and the summertime game. Americans love the sport and are loyal fans to their home teams and favorite players. If you love baseball, then I recommend a summer family trip to Cooperstown, New York. This all-American town is home to the Baseball Hall of Fame. You will be delighted by this small town and the wonderful baseball museum.

The Great Smoky Mountains National Park is the destination for a great summer family vacation. I live nearby the park in Georgia so I have had many adventures in this pristine park during my lifetime. There are two towns on opposite ends of the park that everyone must visit: Gatlinburg, Tennessee, and Cherokee, North Carolina. Gatlinburg is the gateway to the Smoky Mountains. This charming town is filled with shops and restaurants. You always feel welcome as the locals share their Southern hospitality. Cherokee is home to the Cherokee Indian Reservation. The Indian lifestyle is preserved with live demonstrations and the Museum of the Cherokee Indian. The national park is a beautiful place with mountain views and many rivers and streams.

I've traveled to forty-one states and sailed on a ship around the world. But my all-time favorite destination is a beach town located on Florida's Gulf Coast. Panama City Beach, Florida, is my favorite place on earth after my home. The white, sugary, sand beaches are the most beautiful in the world. The water of the Gulf of Mexico is colored with emerald green and many shades of blue. You must visit this beautiful place. Panama City Beach is a place where I can relax. The beach is a wonderful place to pray and meditate. The awesome power of God and the beauty of His earthly creation is so clear with the water, sand, and sunshine. I take long walks on the beach. The sea breeze and sunshine are so refreshing. I watch the waves and collect seashells. I read books and take long naps. I enjoy time with my family and friends and remember how good and special life really is in God's world.

Hembree summer vacation trip to Yellowstone National Park.

The Hembree boy's climb up Mt. Washburn to touch the snow.

Hembree family in the Yellowstone River Canyon.

Hembree family vacation trip to Niagara Falls.

Favorite destination is Panama City Beach, Florida.

For where two or three gather in my name, there I am with them.
—Matthew 18:20 (NIV)

Go therefore and make disciples of all nations, baptizing them in the name of the
Father and of the Son and of the Holy Spirit. Teaching them to observe all that I
have commanded you. And behold, I am with you always, to the end of the age.
—Matthew 28:19–20 (ESV)

And I tell you, you are Peter, and on this rock, I will build my
church, and the gates of hell shall not prevail against it.
—Matthew 16:18 (ESV)

Well, my brothers and sisters, let's summarize. When you meet together, one will sing, another
will teach, another will tell some special revelation God has given, one will speak in tongues,
and another will interpret what is said. But everything that is done must strengthen all of you.
—1 Corinthians 14:26 (NLT)

Speaking to yourselves in psalms and hymns and spiritual songs, singing and making melody
in your heart to the Lord; Giving thanks always for all things unto God and the Father in the
name of the Lord Jesus Christ; Submitting yourselves one to another in the fear of God.
—Ephesians 5:19–21 (KJV 1900)

Keep watch over yourselves and all the flock of which the Holy Spirit has made you
overseers. Be shepherds of the church of God, which he bought with his own blood.
—Acts 20:28 (NIV)

> Then the church throughout Judea, Galilee and Samaria enjoyed a
> time of peace and was strengthened. Living in the fear of the Lord and
> encouraged by the Holy Spirit, it increased in numbers.
> —Acts 9:31 (NIV)

> Is anyone among you sick? Let him call for the elders of the church, and let
> them pray over him, anointing him with oil in the name of the Lord.
> —James 5:14 (ESV)

The church is the body of Christ and the foundation of His ministry in our world. The church is a very important place for Christians to come together and worship our Lord and Savior. Jesus tells His followers to regularly come together to remember and celebrate His death with the Lord's Supper. The church is shared by all members of the community to partake and remember Jesus through Holy Communion. The church celebrates the Lord's Supper and publicly proclaims the death and resurrection of Christ.

> I believe in God, the Father Almighty. Creator of heaven and earth, and in Jesus Christ, His only Son, our Lord, who was conceived by the Holy Spirit, born of the Virgin Mary, suffered under Pontius Pilate, was crucified, died and was buried; He descended into hell; on the third day He rose again from the dead; He ascended into heaven, and is seated at the right hand of God the Father Almighty; from there He will come to judge the living and the dead. I believe in the Holy Spirit, the holy Catholic Church, the communion of Saints, the forgiveness of sins, the resurrection of the body, and life everlasting. (The Apostles' Creed)

Bill attended Flint Hill Methodist Church and was baptized here at the age of 16. Years later, an arsonist set the church on fire, and it was destroyed.

For God so loved the world, that he gave his only Son, that whoever
believes in him should not perish but have eternal life.
—John 3:16 (ESV)

The Lord is my shepherd; I shall not want.
He makes me lie down in green pastures.
He leads me beside still waters.
He restores my soul.
He leads me in paths of righteousness for his name's sake.
Even though I walk through the valley of the shadow of death,
I will fear no evil, for you are with me; your rod and your staff, they comfort me.
You prepare a table before me in the presence of my enemies;
You anoint my head with oil; my cup overflows.
Surely goodness and mercy shall follow me all the days of my life,
And I shall dwell in the house of the Lord forever.
—Psalm 23:1–6 (ESV)

The Beatitudes
Blessed are the poor in spirit: for theirs is the kingdom of heaven.
Blessed are they that mourn: for they shall be comforted.
Blessed are the meek: for they shall inherit the earth.
Blessed are they which do hunger and thirst for righteousness: for they shall be filled.
Blessed are the merciful: for they shall obtain mercy.
Blessed are the pure in heart: for they shall see God.
Blessed are the peacemakers: for they shall be called the children of God.
Blessed are they which are persecuted for righteousness' sake: for theirs is the kingdom of heaven.
Blessed are ye, when men shall revile you, and persecute you, and
say all manner of evil against you falsely, for my sake.

Rejoice, and be exceedingly glad: for great is your reward in heaven:
for so persecuted they the prophets which were before you.
—Matthew 5:3–12 (KJV)

The Lord's Prayer
After this manner therefore pray ye:
Our Father which art in heaven, Hallowed be thy name.
Thy kingdom come. Thy will be done in earth, as it is in heaven.
Give us this day our daily bread.
And forgive us our debts, as we forgive our debtors.
And lead us not into temptation, but deliver us from the evil.
For thine is the kingdom, and the power, and the glory, forever. Amen.
—Matthew 6:9–13 (KJV)

I have discovered this principle of life, that when I want to do what is right, I inevitably do
what is wrong. I love God's law with all my heart. But there is another power within me
that is at war with my mind. This power makes me a slave to the sin that is still within me.
Oh, what a miserable person I am! Who will free me from this life that is dominated by sin
and death? Thank God! The answer is in Jesus Christ our Lord. So you see how it is: In my
mind I really want to obey God's law, but because of my sinful nature I am a slave to sin.
—Romans 7:21–25 (NLT)

Whoever pursues righteousness and love finds life, prosperity, and honor.
—Proverbs 21:21 (NIV)

For there is one God and one mediator between God and mankind, the man Christ Jesus.
—1 Timothy 2:5 (NIV)

Have I not commanded you? Be strong and courageous. Do not be afraid; do not
be discouraged, for the Lord your God will be with you wherever you go.
—Joshua 1:9 (NIV)

Do not be anxious about anything, but in every situation, by prayer and
petition, with thanksgiving, present your request to God.
—Philippians 4:6 (NIV)

Give all your worries and cares to God, for He cares about you.
—1 Peter 5:7 (NLT)

And we know that in all things God works for the good of those who
love him, who have been called according to his purpose.
—Romans 8:28 (NIV)

For I know the plans I have for you, declares the Lord, plans to prosper
you and not to harm you, plans to give you hope in the future.
—Jeremiah 29:11 (NIV)

For the Lord your God is living among you, He is a Mighty Savior.
He will take delight in you with gladness. With his love, He will calm
all your fears. He will rejoice over you with joyful songs.
—Zephaniah 3:17 (NLT)

I have told you these things, so that in me you may have peace. In this world
you will have trouble. But take heart! I have overcome the world.
—John 16:33 (NIV)

If you declare with your mouth, Jesus is Lord, and believe in your
heart that God raised him from the dead, you will be saved.
—Romans 10:9 (NIV)

So do not fear, for I am with you; do not be dismayed, for I am your God. I will
strengthen you and help you; I will uphold you with my righteous right hand.
—Isaiah 41:10 (NIV)

JESUS, THE GREAT PHYSICIAN

I believe in miracles. I believe that Jesus performed miracles two thousand years ago, and I believe Jesus performs miracles today. If you are sick or have medical conditions that plague your body, Jesus can heal you. We must ask for healing through constant prayer. Jesus will answer our prayers and heal our bodies. The most important thing we can do is have faith. Release your worries and have faith in Jesus to heal you.

> So he came again to Cana in Galilee, where he had made the water wine. And at Capernaum there was an official who son was ill. When this man heard that Jesus had come from Judea to Galilee, he went to him and ask him to come down and heal his son, for he was at the point of death. So Jesus said to him, unless you see signs and wonders you will not believe. The official said to him, Sir, come down before my child dies. Jesus said to him, go; your son will live. The man believed the word that Jesus spoke to him and went on his way. As he was going down, his servants met him and told him that his son was recovering. So he asked them the hour when he began to get better, and they said to him, yesterday at the seventh hour the fever left him. The father knew that was the hour when Jesus had said to him, your son will live. And he himself believed, and all his household. This was now the second miracle that Jesus did when he had come from Judea to Galilee. (John 4:46–54 ESV)

Have faith, and pray to Jesus to heal your body.

> And he arose and left the synagogue and entered Simon Peter's house. Now Simon Peter's mother-in-law was ill with fever, and they appealed to him on her behalf. And he stood over her and rebuked the fever, and it left her, and immediately she rose and began to serve them. (Luke 4:38–39 ESV)

Have faith, and pray to Jesus to heal your body.

> That evening at sundown they brought to him all who were sick or oppressed by demons. And the whole city was gathered together at the door. And he healed many who were sick with various diseases, and cast out many demons. And he would not permit the demons to speak, because they knew him. (Mark 1:32–34 ESV)

Have faith, and pray to Jesus to heal your body.

> When he came down from the mountain, great crowds followed him. And behold, a leper came to him and knelt before him, saying Lord, if you will, you can make me clean. And Jesus stretched out his hand and touched him, saying, I will; be clean. And immediately his leprosy was cleansed. (Matthew 8:1–3 ESV)

Have faith, and pray to Jesus to heal your body.

> After he had finished all his sayings in the hearing of the people, he entered Capernaum. Now a centurion had a servant who was sick and at the point of death, who was highly valued by him. When the centurion heard about Jesus, he sent to him elders of the Jews, asking him to come and heal his servant. And when they came to Jesus, they pleaded with him earnestly, saying, he is worthy to have you do this for him, for he loves our nation, and he is the one who built us our synagogue. And Jesus went to them. When he was not far from the house, the centurion sent friends, saying to him, Lord, do not trouble yourself, for I am not worthy to have you come under my roof. Therefore, I did not presume to come to you. But say the word, and let my servant be healed. For I too am a man set under authority, with soldiers under me: and I say to one, go and he goes; and to another, come, and he comes; and to my servant, do this, and he does it. When Jesus heard these things, he marveled at him, and turning to the crowd that followed him, said, I tell you, not even in Israel have I found such faith. And when those who had been sent returned to the house, they found the servant healed. (Luke 7:1–10 ESV)

Have faith, and pray to Jesus to heal your body.

> And behold, some men were bringing on a bed a man who was paralyzed, and they were seeking to bring him in and lay him before Jesus, but finding no way to bring him in, because of the crowd, they went up on the roof and let him down with his

bed through the tiles into the midst before Jesus. And when he saw their faith, he said, man, your sins are forgiven you. (Luke 5:18–20 ESV)

Have faith, and pray to Jesus to heal your body.

Just then a woman who had suffered for twelve years with constant bleeding came up behind him. She touched the fringe of his robe, for she thought, if I can just touch his robe, I will be healed. Jesus turned around, and when he saw her he said, daughter, be encouraged! Your faith has made you well. And the woman was healed at that moment. (Matthew 9:20–22 NLT)

Have faith, and pray to Jesus to heal your body.

And as Jesus passed on from there, two blind men followed him, crying aloud, have mercy on us, Son of David. When he entered the house, the blind men came to him, and Jesus said to them, do you believe that I am able to do this? They said to him, yes, Lord. Then he touched their eyes, saying, according to your faith be it done to you. And their eyes were opened. And Jesus sternly warned them, see that no one knows about it. But they went away and spread his fame to all the land. (Matthew 9:27–31 ESV)

Have faith, and pray to Jesus to heal your body.

Now there in Jerusalem by the Sheep Gate a pool, in Aramaic called Bethesda, which had five roofed colonnades. In these lay a multitude of invalids, blind, lame and paralyzed. One man was there who had been an invalid for thirty-eight years. When Jesus saw him lying there and knew that he had already been there a long time, he said to him, do you want to be healed? The sick man answered him, Sir, I have no one to put me into the pool when the water is stirred up, and while I am going another steps down before me. Jesus said to him, get up, take up your bed, and walk. And at once the man was healed, and he took up his bed and walked. Now that day was the Sabbath. (John 5:2–9 ESV)

Have faith, and pray to Jesus to heal your body.

When they crossed over the lake, they came to land at Gennesaret and moored to the shore. And when they got out of the boat, the people immediately recognized him and ran about the whole region and began to bring the sick people on their beds to wherever they heard he was. And wherever he came, in villages, cities, or countryside, they laid the sick in the marketplaces and implored him that they might touch even the fringe of his garment. And as many as touched it were healed and made well. (Mark 6:53–56 ESV)

Have faith, and pray to Jesus to heal your body.

And they brought to him a man who was deaf and had a speech impediment, and they begged him to lay his hands on him. And taking him aside from the crowd privately, he put his fingers into his ears, and after spitting touched his tongue. And looking up to heaven, he sighed and said to him, Ephphatha, that is, be opened. And his ears were opened, his tongue was released, he was healed and spoke plainly. (Mark 7:32–35 ESV)

Have faith, and pray to Jesus to heal your body.

And they came to Bethsaida. And some people brought to him a blind man and begged him to touch him. And he took the blind man by the hand and led him out of the village, and when he had spit on his eyes and laid his hands on him, he asked him, do you see anything? And he looked up and said, I see people, but they look like trees, walking. Then Jesus laid his hands on his eyes again; and he opened his eyes, his sight was restored, and he saw everything clearly. (Mark 8:22–25 ESV)

Have faith, and pray to Jesus to heal your body.

And behold, there was a woman who had had a disabling spirit for eighteen years. She was bent over and could not fully straighten herself. When Jesus saw her, he called her over and said to her, Woman, you are freed from your disability. And he laid his hands on her, and immediately she was made straight, and she glorified God. (Luke 13:11–13 ESV)

Have faith, and pray to Jesus to heal your body.

As he drew near to Jericho, a blind man was sitting by the roadside begging. And hearing a crowd going by, he inquired what this meant. They told him; Jesus of Nazareth is passing by. And he cried out, Jesus, Son of David, have mercy on me! And those who were in front rebuked him, telling him to be silent. But he cried out all the more, Son of David, have mercy on me! And Jesus stopped and commanded him to be brought to him. What do you want me to do for you? He said, Lord, let me recover my sight. And Jesus said to him, recover your sight; your faith has made you well. And immediately he recovered his sight and followed him, glorifying God, and all the people, when they saw it, gave praise to God. (Luke 18:35–43 ESV)

Jesus is the Great Physician, so have faith and pray to him to heal your body.

GOD CAN HEAL YOU

God can heal your body from sickness and disease. Physical and mental illness are often caused by the internal and environmental darkness of our world. The foods and drinks we consume and the mental stress we encounter each day can lead to sickness and disease. Our bodies are exposed to deadly chemicals in our foods and drinks that cause cancer and other terrible diseases. Our immune systems are compromised by the overmedication of drugs. The natural balance inside our bodies is damaged and weakened as our immune system tries to fight and kill infectious diseases and viruses that attack our bodies.

There is a war taking place inside us and around us. Both seen and unseen viruses and diseases plague our world. But there is hope and a way to save yourself from the physical and mental dangers we encounter every day. Our God, the only God, whose power and grace control the universe, can save you. God can heal you. God can heal your pain and agony. God can heal your mind and your body. God can heal your heart and broken body to give you peace. Pray to God, and read these verses from the Bible as you ask for divine healing. God wants to help you, guide you, and have a relationship with you. As you read the following verses from the Bible, open your heart and mind, and ask God to place his healing hand upon you.

> He personally carried our sins in his body on the cross so that we can be dead to sin and live for what is right. By his wounds you are healed. (1 Peter 2:24 NLT)

My God, hear my prayer. Heal my body from sickness and disease.

> He sent out his word and healed them, and delivered them from their destructions. (Psalm 107:20 NKJV)

My God, hear my prayer. Heal my body from sickness and disease.

No harm will come to you. No sickness will come near your house. He will put his angels in charge of you to protect you in all your ways. (Psalm 91:10–11 God's Word Translation)

My God, hear my prayer. Heal my body from sickness and disease.

This fulfilled the word of the Lord through the prophet Isaiah, who said, He took our sicknesses and removed our diseases. (Matthew 8:17 NLT)

My God, hear my prayer. Heal my body from sickness and disease.

You should know that your body is a temple for the Holy Spirit who is in you. You have received the Holy Spirit from God. So you do not belong to yourselves. (1 Corinthians 6:19 NCV)

My God, hear my prayer. Heal my body from sickness and disease.

It is the spirit that gives life. The flesh doesn't give life. The words I told you are spirit, and they give life. (John 6:63 NCV)

My God, hear my prayer. Heal my body from sickness and disease.

A peaceful heart leads to a healthy body; jealousy is like cancer in the bones. (Proverbs 14:30 NLT)

My God, hear my prayer. Heal my body from sickness and disease.

You must serve only the Lord your God. If you do, I will bless your food and water. I will take away sickness from you. (Exodus 23:25 NLT)

My God, hear my prayer. Heal my body from sickness and disease.

I will not die; instead, I will live and tell what the Lord has done. (Psalm 118:17 NLT)

My God, hear my prayer. Heal my body from sickness and disease.

Let all that I am praise the Lord; may I never forget the good things he does for me. He forgives all my sins and heals all my diseases. He redeems me from death and crowns me with love and tender mercies. He fills my life with good things. My youth is renewed like the Eagle's! (Psalm 103:2–5 NLT)

My God, hear my prayer. Heal my body from sickness and disease.

The thief's purpose is to steal and kill and destroy. My purpose is to give them a rich and satisfying life. (John 10:10 NLT)

My God, hear my prayer. Heal my body from sickness and disease.

You can ask for anything in my name, and I will do it, so that the Son can bring glory to the Father. Yes, ask me for anything in my name, and I will do it! (John 14:13–14 NLT)

My God, hear my prayer. Heal my body from sickness and disease.

So I tell you to believe that you have received the things you ask for in prayer, and God will give them to you. (Mark 11:24 NCV)

My God, hear my prayer. Heal my body from sickness and disease.

A happy heart is like good medicine, but a broken spirit drains your strength. (Proverbs 17:22 NCV)

My God, hear my prayer. Heal my body from sickness and disease.

My child, pay attention to my words; listen closely to what I say. Don't ever forget my words; keep them always in mind. They are the key to life for those who find them; they bring health to the whole body. (Proverbs 4:20–22 NCV)

My God, hear my prayer. Heal my body from sickness and disease.

There is life in doing what is right. Along that path you will never die. (Proverbs 12:28 New International Reader's Version, 1998 ed.)

My God, hear my prayer. Heal my body from sickness and disease.

Moses was 120 years old when he died. His eyesight never became poor, and he never lost his physical strength. (Deuteronomy 34:7 GW)

My God, hear my prayer. Heal my body from sickness and disease.

> For the sin of this one man, Adam, caused death to rule over many. But even greater is God's wonderful grace and his gift of righteousness, for all who receive it will live in triumph over sin and death through this one man, Jesus Christ. (Romans 5:17 NLT)

My God, hear my prayer. Heal my body from sickness and disease.

THE FACE OF GOD

My God will save me.
My God will save me.
My God will save me.
Blessed be Your name.
I am a weak and dreadful sinner trapped in sinful ways.
You lift me up from darkness and carry me every day.
You fill my heart with love.
You are my heavenly angel guiding me from above.
I love You, Lord, with all my heart and with all my strength and mind.
You love me too. I know You do. You are so sweet and kind.
The Holy Spirit is in my heart, and Jesus died for me.
You are the only God the world should know; Your truth has set me free.
All we need are faith, hope, and love to carry us through life.
We must turn away from darkness and follow You, our light.
You are my God, my heavenly light.
You are my God, my heavenly light.
You are my God, my heavenly light.
Eternal life in heaven is Your gift to me. It is the path that I will take.
You are the way, the truth, and the life. Let us follow You for goodness' sake.
You have blessed me and forgiven me. You know my sinful ways.
I love my life and feel its worth.
My desire is to offer peace and goodwill to all I encounter here on earth.
A long time from now when my work is done on earth,
I long to see You and be in Your light, my God, to touch Your face,
To spend eternity with You joined together in Your heavenly place.
I long to touch Your face, my God.
I long to touch Your face.
I long to touch Your face, my God.
I long to touch Your face.
Eternal life in heaven will be a wonderful place.
Salvation for a sinner is Your amazing grace.

HELLO, BETH

You caught my eye a long time ago.

Your pretty face caused my heart to overflow.

Those high school days were fun and free.

You sat in the hallway as a storm passed by us.

You looked my way, and I couldn't believe you noticed me.

Beth, you take my breath away.

Oh Beth, you take my breath away.

Beth, you take my breath away.

Oh Beth, you take my breath away.

Your kiss, and your touch, made me love you so much.

Our hearts would race every time we embraced.

I can't stop holding you, because I know your love is true.

Your life is full of kindness, and it is there to remind us of a special girl that is you.

Beth, you are the girl for me.

Beth, your love has lifted me.

Beth, you have completed my life.

Beth, I finally made you my wife.

We laughed, and we cried, as the years passed by.

Three sons are our gift from God above.

They have filled our life with joy and love.

I loved you then, and I love you now.

Your pretty face always makes me smile.

Oh Beth, I will love you forever.

Because a love like ours will keep us together.

Beth Hembree during our first year of marriage.

MONTA RAYE

There was a sweet girl named Monta Raye.

She was born in the mountains faraway.

Freckles on her face and pretty blonde hair, her skin was so soft and really quite fair.

Her mother was Martha and loved her so much.

She couldn't keep her, because times were so tough.

The Great Depression was a hard time for everyone.

It was especially tough for a little one.

Grandma and Grandpa raised that sweet little girl.

She was loved and cared for each and every day.

She was safe and secure in a special way.

Martha, Dale, Andrea, and Monta Raye left their home in North Carolina one warm spring day.

They traveled to Georgia and settled in Fairplay.

Georgia was their new home, and they were happy to stay.

Her nickname was Speedy on the basketball team.

As a Douglas County graduate, she accomplished her dream.

It was a hot summer day at Johnson's swimming pool.

She met a boy who was out of school.

A love affair was in the air.

Aubrey Herman Hembree was the name of her man.

He loved her and held her close as they walked hand in hand.

A wedding day happened at the Middle Courthouse.

They traveled to the mountains for a honeymoon escape.

Sharing the good news with Grandma was a visit they had to make.

Their first home was nothing more than an old chicken house.

Herman quickly learned Monta Raye needed another house.

Post Road was their final destination.

They bought a house on a hill and started wonderful family relations.

Starting a family was their greatest desire.

Five children were a blessing from God above.

This home was filled with joy, happiness, and love.

Arubra, Phil, Johnny, Vista, and Bill.

The children are guided by faith, hope, and goodwill.

The happiness ended with a tragedy one day.

Aubrey Herman's heart stopped and he passed away.

His spirit was strong, and he lives in our hearts each day.

Monta Raye cried and was alone. How could it all end this way?

Her faith in God lifted her spirits up high.

She gathered her children and promised she would not die.

She worked two jobs for eighteen years.

Long days and nights with a lot of tears.

A lunchroom lady in Winston school. A waitress at Rock Inn.

She retired from Winn-Dixie, and her working days would finally end.

She loved her children and guided them along life's way.

She wanted them near her and begged them, "Please stay."

She listened to Elvis and passed the time away.

His music filled her loneliness and lifted her up each day.

She flirted with men because she loved them all so much.

Her words made us laugh and smile and such.

Elvis was always her favorite man.

But when she met Kevin Costner, she became his biggest fan.

We never really knew what she just might say.

She loved all of life and lived it just that way.

Her name was so beautiful, we called her Monta Raye.

Her life was filled with struggles and strife.

But her happiness and good spirit showed us she loved her life.

What we keep in memory is ours unchanged forever.

Monta Raye will be with us in our hearts each day.

She will fill our memory today and forever.

Monta Raye Hembree meeting actor Kevin Costner in Monterey, California.

USA

The United States of America.
Freedom is what we are here for.
Freedom is what we live for.
Freedom is what they died for.
Let us all be free.
There is no other place where I want to be,
But living in a land that is free.
It can work for you and me.
We must have faith in God above
Because He gave us this land to love.
The United States of America.
The United States of America.
The United States of America.
Our home from sea to sea.
We can't forget our history.
The past can't erase our destiny.
We all long for being free, so leave it alone and let it be.
Change is all around us and will usually only confound us.
The socialists want to control us.
The communists want to destroy us.
The dictators want to lead us
And take away our right to be free.
The United States of America.
The United States of America.
The United States of America.
It is the best place for you and me.
We the people have formed this union.
Let's stay together and protect our freedom.
United we are strong, and the bond we share is never wrong.
So let's have a celebration for our home this incredible nation.
Red, white, and blue,
I will always stand for you.
Red, white, and blue,

The United States stands for all that is true.
So join me now and I will show you how to celebrate and stand for freedom
Because we are the United States of America,
From sea to shining sea.
Stand up for America, stand high.
Stand up for America, stand high.
Stand up for America, stand high.
I will stand up for America until I die.
USA, USA, USA.

Bill Hembree wins the prestigious United States Air Force Spirit of America Award.

GEORGIA

Georgia is a special place. I love to call it home.

Atlanta is our capital, beneath the big, gold dome.

The city is a worldly place; the airport keeps it growing.

The people of Georgia are its greatest gift; they always keep it glowing.

The Blue Ridge Mountains rise high to touch the sky.

Crashing waves from the ocean touch the Golden Isles and it is a beautiful sight to see.

Savannah was our first port town.

Fountains and live oak trees with Spanish moss can be seen all around.

Columbus, Albany, and Macon are great towns to visit.

There is so much to see in each place, you don't want to miss it.

Augusta is a famous town; the golf world holds it dearly.

Springtime at the Masters brings cheers to us yearly.

Pine trees grow almost everywhere; they are a beautiful sight to see.

Growing high in the sky, they look like a tower.

The brown thrasher is our state bird, and the Cherokee Rose is our state flower.

Georgia is the Peach State, and everyone loves its sweet taste.

Peanuts, chickens, and onions make our farmers so great.

Georgia is a beautiful state with so much a person can do.

Fishing, hunting, biking, and hiking or almost anything just for you.

Football with the Bulldogs in Athens and baseball with the Braves.

Spending time with family and friends always makes a special day.

Georgia was an original state, and 1776 gave us our freedom.

Wisdom, Justice, and Moderation are the foundations of who we are.

In God we trust all things, and that is what makes Georgia a shining star.

Georgia Capitol where Bill served as a State Representative for eighteen years.

FLORIDA

There is this special place I know.

Its land is always free from snow.

The sunshine rises up so high and warms our days with a sunny sky.

We love the beach and its soft, white sand.

The waves are calm as they touch the land.

The water turns blue and green all day.

The warm waves make it a perfect place to play.

This place you know, it's Florida.

This place you know, it's Florida.

This place you know, it's Florida.

Its beauty is for all to see.

Having fun in the sun makes it a special place just for you and me.

Deep-sea fishing is the best place to be.

Catching grouper and snapper and marlin too, bonita and wahoo make a story for you.

Your sailboat can catch the wind and glide,

While your fishing boat and speedboat are a fast and smooth ride.

Florida is the Sunshine State.

Florida is the Sunshine State.

Florida is the Sunshine State.

Just being here makes me feel so great.

Walking along the beach each day is a peaceful way to pass some time.

A margarita in hand with a twist of lime.

My toes in the sand and a good book in hand.

Just relax; there is no need for a plan.

The joy and laughter of children who play—

Building sandcastles brings them happiness that lasts all day.

Palm trees and seashells and soft, white sand, sunshine and a sea breeze make me love this land.

Florida is the place for me.

Florida is where I long to be.

Florida warms my soul as I grow old.

Water, water everywhere; it's a beautiful sight to see.

The ocean waves will rise and fall from sea to shining sea.

Red skies in the morning are a sailor's warning, and red skies at night are sailor's delight.

Sailing across the water so blue,
Sailing is what I have longed to do.
Sailing along the coast all day,
Sailing under the stars and moonlight all night.
Take me away to Florida.
Take me away to the beach.
Take me away to Florida.
It's a place I long to reach.
Sunshine and happiness to fill my days.
Take me away to Florida, I pray.

Florida sunset.

BEER

Give me another beer, my dear.
Give me another beer.
You have left me here all alone
As I drink my sorrows to the bone.
Give me another beer, my dear.
Give me another beer.
I don't need you anymore.
My friends all say I was better off before.
Give me another beer, my dear.
Give me another beer.
You took my money when I called you Honey.
Now I'm broke and all alone.
You took my truck and you took my home.
I'm sitting here, and you are gone.
Give me another beer, my dear.
Give me another beer.
The bartender listened to me all night long.
He said I was right and you were wrong.
I played the jukebox and sang a song
To help me forget you and move along.
Give me another beer, my dear.
Give me another beer.
My life is no good; it's upside down.
I'm stuck here, and you left town.
My friends all say things will get better now.
I shake my head because I can't see how.
Give me another beer, my dear.
Give me another beer.
I am lonesome and my heart is broke.
There is nothing left. Let's have a smoke.
I'm moving on because I am strong.
My mind will soon be clear.
I'm better off without you, dear.

The drinks are on me.
Let's have more beer.
Give me another beer, my dear.
Give me another beer.
Give me another beer, my dear.
Give me another beer.

GRADUATION

Our time has come.
Our work is done.
Our days and nights of studying are gone.
It is time to cheer
And celebrate this year.
Our teachers and professors are so proud!
As we cry with joy and sing out loud.
Sing this song for all the world to hear.
Graduate and celebrate!
Graduate and celebrate!
Graduate and celebrate!
We passed our tests to graduate and our essays are complete.
Life is good, I feel good, the world is really sweet.
Thank you for the memories and the friendships we embrace.
This is our time to graduate.
This is our time to celebrate.
This is our time to change the world.
This is our time to take a stand.
This is our time to come together and make this world so much better.
Remember my name, and remember my face.
Remember all the good times we had at this place.
Let's have a party here.
Let's have a party there.
Let the celebration fill the air.
Let's graduate and celebrate.
Let's graduate and celebrate.
Happy times are here!

Bill's Douglas County high school graduation in the Spring of 1984.

I am thankful for living on Thanksgiving.
Thankful for my family, friends, and all.
Thankful to them for us having a ball.
We are gathered around the table, ready to eat.
The turkey and dressing are now complete.
But first we must thank God and all His creations
And for keeping peace throughout the nations.

Trouble Coming

Life is a roller coaster with ups and downs. Every day we face challenges that make us happy so we can celebrate or sadness that tears our world apart. We can't hide from our problems so it is important that we live life fully and enjoy every moment of every day. We live in a world created by God that is filled with beauty and splendor. If we open our eyes, we can clearly see the majesty of His creation.

The lyrics of a song by Louis Armstrong called "What a Wonderful World" describe the beauty of God's gift to all of us every day.

I see skies of blue.
And clouds of white.
The bright blessed day.
The dark sacred night.
And I think to myself.
What a wonderful world.

It was a gray Sunday morning on November 5, 2017, for me. My wife, Beth, and I had dinner at a Mexican restaurant Saturday night and I woke up at 3 a.m. with a stomachache. I didn't wake

Beth because I thought it would pass. But hour after hour of tossing and turning, the pain did not go away. At sunrise, Beth was very concerned about my condition, but I assured her if I just remained in bed, the pain would eventually go away.

The stomach pain never stopped, and around midday, fever struck my body. At this point, Beth wasted no more time. She loaded me up in the car and drove me to the Piedmont Hospital emergency room in Atlanta. My primary doctor practiced at the Piedmont Hospital Medical Center, which held all of my medical records, so this seemed like the appropriate place to go for emergency medical help.

I've always believed that God places guardian angels in our presence to guard us and protect us. I've always said to be kind to everyone because you never know if that someone is an angel. As we walked into the emergency room, Beth was at the counter checking me in and I sat alone in the waiting room. I felt horrible as the fever raged in my body and my stomach pain increased. Suddenly an elderly woman appeared in front of me. She didn't have a uniform on, but I thought she worked for the hospital. I didn't say anything to her because I didn't feel like talking, but she smiled at me. During the rush to leave home and get to the hospital, I put on my shoes but didn't tie the laces. This remarkable woman knelt down in front of me and tied both of my shoes. She then took my hand and with a smile on her face told me that everything was going to be OK. Then she was gone. I believe she was an angel sent by God to comfort me and give me peace. This simple act of tying my shoelaces reminded me of when Jesus washed His disciples' feet. Show love and kindness to those in need, and be humble before God.

I was immediately checked into an emergency room, where the doctors and nurses performed a wide range of tests to determine my condition. After reviewing the CT scan and blood work, the doctor determined that I had appendicitis. The scans showed a partial rupture of my swollen appendix, and emergency surgery was needed with no time to waste.

I kissed Beth goodbye and was rushed back to the emergency room. The doctors and medical team performed an appendectomy. It is hard to believe that this tiny organ called the appendix could cause so much pain and trauma in my body. Some have said that the appendix plays no useful role in the body and should be removed before problems develop. My appendix was now gone, and the fever and stomach pain disappeared. I was in recovery and checked in the hospital for an overnight stay so I could be monitored safely.

The doctors met with Beth and said the surgery was successful. The doctors had some concern about the appendix. They told my wife that the appendix was an unusual green color. This gangrene-swollen appendix would be sent to pathology for further review.

This was the first sign of trouble.

CANCER: THE WORST DAY EVER

Friday, November 17, 2017, turned out to be the worst day of my life. The day started out normally with a routine follow-up with my doctors after the appendix surgery. The doctor's appointment was at 11 a.m. in Atlanta so Beth and I decided to make it a fun day for the family. We invited our sons Thomas and Miles along and made reservations for lunch at our favorite Japanese restaurant, Benihana.

We arrived at the medical center near Piedmont Hospital for my appointment. I was called back from the waiting room to meet with the doctor. Beth and the boys stayed behind to wait for me. I sat down on the medical table in the office and noticed that the doctor and nurse seemed very reserved with their emotions. It was very different from the normal feeling of "We are happy to see you and things are looking good."

The doctor said to me that although the appendix surgery was successful, the pathology report was bad. The green-colored appendix that had been removed from my body was sent to the pathology medical team for review and analysis. The doctor said, "Their findings tell us that you have cancer. A cancerous tumor was inside your appendix, causing the green color, and it broke through the wall of your appendix and spread mucus-type cancer cells into your abdomen."

I fell back on the table in disbelief. *Cancer* is the worst word you ever want to hear from a doctor. I lay there silently for a few seconds, but it seemed like hours. I thought, *Am I going to die from cancer? Whenever I hear the word* cancer, *I think of death because so many people I knew died from it. Why is this happening to me? I can't die and leave my family. I'm a healthy man who takes care of himself. I don't drink, I don't smoke, I exercise, and I always avoid making foolish, life-threatening decisions. I always expected to live a long life. I actually prayed that I would live to be 103 by playing it safe for You and me. The most important thing to me in my life is family. I want to grow old with Beth and experience the celebrations of life with her. I always dreamed of watching my sons graduate from college and start their careers with the celebration. I dream of my sons meeting that special girl who would become their partner for life. I am an ordained minister and dream of being a part of my sons' weddings. Beth and I love babies and I dream of holding and loving my grandchildren.*

The word *cancer* shattered all of these hopes and dreams in seconds.

I lifted myself back up from the table and looked at the doctor, feeling sick inside. I asked if we could bring Beth back so he could share this news with her.

The doctor informed her that I had cancer, and she was overwhelmed with emotions and started to cry. I asked the doctor what I should do, and he said, "You need to find a surgical oncologist. Surgery is the best course of action at this stage of having cancer. You need a surgical procedure called a hemicolectomy where six inches of your colon connected to the appendix is cut away and removed." He said, "If the surgery is successful and the cancerous contaminated area is removed, you may have a healthy long life. But if the cancer has spread, you will need to undergo chemotherapy treatments." He said, "Cancer reoccurrence will be a lifelong battle for you. Even with surgery and chemotherapy, there may always be one tiny cancer cell floating in your body, avoiding your immune system, waiting to strike you again with sickness and death.

Beth and I left the doctor's office in a state of shock. We tried to hold back our emotions because Thomas and Miles were with us. We all sat in the car inside the parking deck. I sat next to Beth, trying to find the right words to say and the appropriate meaning of what was happening in our lives. I told the boys that we have a strong, loving family that can overcome any challenge. Our faith in God and our love for one another will overcome any obstacle in life. I told them the doctor had diagnosed me with cancer but not to worry because there were options to cure the cancer. I told them we need to stay positive and follow the doctor's direction. We had never experienced anything like this, but our journey together would carry the day with good health and happiness.

WHERE CAN I FIND A CANCER DOCTOR?

When you are faced with a life-threatening disease, the news is so overwhelming that it is difficult to regain your composure and make wise decisions. Your judgment is clouded by so many emotional thoughts. Logically, the first step is to find a good doctor who can treat your disease. Daily prayer is the foundation of my day when I ask God for wisdom and common sense to guide me in all my decisions. The devil and his evil darkness fill your mind with fear and hopeless anxiety. The sinful world that we live in plagues our minds with negative thoughts to challenge our faith. If we stay positive and listen to the voice of the Holy Spirit inside us, we can block out the devil and his evil and destructive ways. Pray and ask for help. "Help me, God. Help me, Jesus. Help me, Holy Spirit. Save me and help me find a doctor who can destroy this cancer."

I was so confused and surprised by my diagnosis that I did not know what a cancer doctor was called. I had been healthy and strong so I didn't have a primary doctor to turn to for advice and direction. Beth had been treated by an exceptional primary doctor for years. She described this doctor as the most thoughtful, knowledgeable, and experienced physician who had ever treated her. His name was Dr. Mario J. R. Ravry and we called him for help. He referred us to Dr. Daniel Dubovsky, an oncologist at Northside Hospital in Atlanta.

We quickly made an appointment with Dr. Dubovsky. He had many years of experience and calmed our emotions with a medical plan. He said that immediate surgery for me was the best option to keep the cancer from spreading inside me. A right-side hemicolectomy where the colon is connected to the appendix must be removed. He contacted a surgical oncologist named Dr. Joshua Weiner from Emory University Hospital and explained my medical condition. Dr. Weiner agreed to perform the surgery, and a date was set for January 2, 2018. The surgery was completed, and no evidence of disease was found.

It would take several months for my body to recover from surgery. At that point, Dr. Dubovsky recommended that I begin a traditional chemotherapy protocol to destroy unseen cancer cells in my abdomen. I started three months of chemotherapy cancer treatment in April, May, and June at Northside Hospital Cancer Center. The drugs used were FOLFOX, 5-FU, leucovorin, and oxaliplatin. The traditional side effects of nausea, fatigue, diarrhea, and nerve damage to my hands and feet were all present.

After several months of chemotherapy treatment, one Saturday afternoon in June, I experienced the worst side effect my body had ever encountered. Beth had gone to lunch with a friend so I was home alone. My body began to ache, and I had chills. I could not find any comfort so I wrapped myself in a large blanket and went upstairs to lie down. Beth arrived home soon after and was alarmed by my condition. She took my temperature, and it was 104 degrees Fahrenheit. She called the oncology nurse on duty during the weekend, and the nurse recommended we go to the emergency room for treatment.

The ER doctor ran through a number of test and nothing showed to be abnormal or unusual. My fever was a mystery that no one could solve. After five or six hours of feeling terrible, the fever stopped and my body seemed normal again. The very next day in the afternoon, the fever started all over again. The emergency room doctors had no solution the day before so I decided to endure the pain and discomfort until the fever stopped. For forty days, every afternoon I had a fever in my body that lasted from five to six hours. In my opinion, fever is the worst medical condition someone can endure. I felt like I had the flu every day for forty days with no relief. I saw an infectious disease doctor because there was concern that I had a blood disease. The results were negative. No one could figure out why my body was reacting in this terrible way.

Finally, the doctors decided to end the chemotherapy treatments and remove the infusion port for my body. After forty days of living in misery, the fever stopped. I believe that my body and its immune system were fighting against the chemotherapy drugs and fever is a symptom. I finally had relief from all this pain and suffering.

Hello, everyone. This is Bill. I just turned fifty-five years old, but unfortunately, a few days ago, I received a very difficult diagnosis. I was diagnosed with cancer. It is a very rare cancer called mucinous carcinoma. The cancer is in my abdomen and in the mucus inside my abdomen. I have two tumors on my abdominal wall and one on my diaphragm. So it is early in the stages of cancer and my oncologist will start with chemotherapy for the next four months. Hopefully this will reduce the size of the cancer. It is very difficult to treat because it is in the mucus and moving around the abdominal cavity. In August I will undergo surgery called HIPEC. Surgery will hopefully remove any remaining tumors and also remove any of the remaining cancer cells in my abdomen.

Cancer is such a devastating disease, and it affects so many of us. We all know people in our family or friends and in networks that we know who have cancer. People deal with this disease every day. I want to say to you that the most important thing that a cancer patient can have is a good support group. A supportive, compassionate, and understanding family and friends. So this is why I wanted to tell you about my diagnosis. The difficulties I will face and all of the other people who deal with cancer every day will be hard mentally and physically. I know that fighting cancer is a very difficult process to overcome.

I believe with a positive attitude, with help and motivation from family and friends, and with spiritual guidance, I can win this battle. We all know that we can overcome this disease. So this is the first part of my journey. I have a wonderful family, a supportive wife, and children. It is not only emotional for me; it is very emotional for them as well. The reason for this is when we often hear the word *cancer,* the immediate thought is death. But now there are so many advances with medicine and technology. There are life and hope for people who suffer from all different types of cancer.

The most important thing is that we want to live, we love life, and we want to live. We want to enjoy those moments with our family and friends and to be a part of those life moments. That is the factor that we look forward to and have hope in. To know that we will have a tomorrow and have time to spend with our family and friends. Even though it is going to be difficult, chemotherapy will make me sick. It is a process that we have to go through. The surgery is by no means something that I look forward to, but it is something I must do.

In the end, I know that because of my family, friends, and faith—most of all my family and faith—I will overcome this adversity and the life that is ahead of me will be great with a great future. At the end of the day, we just need to love life and help each other. We need to love one another each and every day. This is the basis of what we are as humans. So my journey is just beginning with this difficult disease. I wanted you to know, to share with you, and to talk with you directly about my emotions. I will keep you updated as I start chemotherapy. I love you all very much, and I look forward to many, many life moments in the future.

ANGELS WATCHING OVER ME

Hi, everyone. This is Bill, and I wanted to give you an update on my cancer diagnosis. The doctors have plans in place to heal me and get my body back in shape. Ultimately my life is in God's hands. As you know, cancer is a terrible disease because it is your own body that is attacking itself. Every day your body produces millions of new cells. Unfortunately, in our bodies with cancer, these cells have gone rogue and have gone bad. Our bodies are producing abnormal cells that are destroying the good cells and are invading different parts of our body. So with chemotherapy, the goal is to try to destroy those bad cancer cells, but unfortunately, they destroy good cells as well.

The doctors have placed me on a regiment for chemotherapy. A PICC line has been surgically placed in my arm; some people use a port that is placed under the skin. The medical team will pump the harsh chemotherapy chemicals through the PICC line into my bloodstream. The PICC line catheter travels to your heart. The chemicals are then circulated throughout the body to try to destroy cancer cells.

The first type of chemotherapy drug that I am taking is called 5FU. The side effects are nausea, digestive issues, mouth sores, and hand and feet rashes. So far, I have only had nausea. The second type of chemotherapy drug that I am taking is called Irinotecan. The side effects with this chemo are hair loss, fatigue, and fever. So far, I have just developed a lot of fatigue. Things are going well and I feel like we are on the right track to recovery. I did have a setback. A blood clot developed in my arm so treatment was stopped. After taking blood thinners for a few weeks, the chemo regiment was started again. Four months of chemo and a two-month break from chemotherapy so my body can recover for surgery.

I want to thank everyone so very much for reaching out to me and my family. We are all grateful for the outpouring of prayers and support. The compassion that you have shown us is so wonderful and encouraging in dealing with my cancer diagnosis. It just shows me the level of spiritual involvement in our lives, and He gives me peace. It gives me peace of mind to know that I have so many angels out there watching over me and praying for me and my family. So many angels are giving me spiritual hope. Angels who are praying that I have a full recovery so I can live a long and productive life.

I want to thank you from the bottom of my heart, and my family does the same because we are truly, *truly* grateful. We never expected this outreach from so many angels. You are also critical to my journey because I can't walk this walk alone. Cancer patients and others who are sick and afflicted need to walk with others because that support is so important. So I am walking with you and I am so grateful that you are walking with me. I love you all and thank you from the bottom of my heart. Walk in faith, and you will never walk alone.

CANCER INFUSION CENTER

Cancer is a terrible disease. The most common treatment for all cancer is chemotherapy drugs. Chemotherapy is a type of cancer treatment that uses one or more anticancer drugs as part of a standardized chemotherapy treatment plan. Chemotherapy is given to patients with the aim of destroying cancer cells and reducing the spread of cancer. Chemotherapy drugs target cells in the body that grow and divide quickly as cancer cells do, causing tumors to grow throughout the body. There are three ways that doctors inject chemotherapy drugs into the body. The first one is a port that is surgically placed in the chest, leading to major veins to deliver the chemotherapy chemicals. The second method is using a PICC line in the arm, also delivering the chemicals through veins in your body. An IV in the arm can also be used to inject the drugs. Not only do the chemotherapy drugs destroy cancer cells, but they also destroy healthy cells, causing many bad side effects that affect your hair, skin, intestines, and bone marrow. Cancer patients are often very sick after chemotherapy treatment because of these harsh side effects. The length of time for chemotherapy treatment can range from five minutes to more than eight hours. Nausea is the most common side effect during chemotherapy infusions.

The cancer infusion center is the medical facility where the chemotherapy treatments take place. The infusion center is usually located in a medical facility near the hospital. Most chemotherapy treatments start early in the day at around 8 a.m. when the nurse begins the process with blood work. The blood work results will be given to the doctor who will determine if your body is able to proceed with the treatment. If your blood counts are too low and your immune system is compromised, treatment will be postponed until your body regains new strength.

The chemicals injected into the body destroy your blood cells, both cancer cells and good blood cells. Your white blood cells are your body's defense mechanism against diseases and viruses. If the chemotherapy chemicals destroy too many white blood cells, your body is in danger to infections. The blood work will show the white blood count, and if the count is too low, the treatment must be canceled.

My doctor meets with me to review all my test results. The plan is to stay on target with four months of chemotherapy and surgery in six months to remove the cancerous tumors. The infusion process takes a long time. My wife and I are at the infusion center for more than six hours for each treatment.

The first chemical I received is a drug called Avastin. The IV injection takes ninety minutes. Avastin destroys the blood supply to the cancer cell, starving it to death. The next chemotherapy I received was a chemotherapy drug called Irinotecan. The IV takes two hours. This drug also destroys the cancer cells in your body. The last chemical I received is a drug called 5 FU. It is a slow pump IV that takes forty-eight hours to inject into your body. I carry this IV bag and pump home, and it will take two days and nights to complete the process before I return to the infusion center to return the pump.

Chemotherapy treatment at the infusion center is a very difficult process mentally and physically. I keep a positive mental attitude to stay strong. I will never give up on life. I will never give up on hope. I will never give up on my faith. I will never give up on living a happy life in this wonderful world. Life is a precious gift, and I will not let cancer destroy it. My body may be damaged by the chemotherapy chemicals, but my heart is filled with peace and love. A strong support group of family and friends is critical for survival with cancer. The prayers and encouragement from others are so important to lift the spirit. Encouragement from others comes in so many ways, and each plays a special part in keeping my spirit and hope alive. Cards, flowers, Bible devotions, phone calls, prayer cards, prayer shirts, text, and prayer blankets are just a few of the many blessings I received from friends and family during my fight to beat cancer. I loved them all and was so grateful that they all love me.

Bill's chemotherapy treatment

H i. This is Bill, and I want to talk to you about the mental battle with cancer. Chemotherapy drugs cause very harsh side effects to your body. Hair loss, fatigue, nausea, rashes, and fever are just a few of the many harsh conditions from these drugs that plague your body. Chemotherapy chemicals are destroying the cancer tumors, but they are also destroying my body.

A few months ago, I was diagnosed with mucinous carcinoma of my abdomen. This is a very rare and aggressive cancer. This cancer is in the mucus that lubricates all the organs of your body like the liver, stomach, pancreas, kidneys, intestines, bladder, and diaphragm. The cancer cells can create tumors on your vital organs, which is very bad and life-threatening. Mucinous carcinoma cancer is so aggressive moving through your abdomen that my doctors are going to treat it as stage 4 cancer.

The medical team working with me took a biopsy of my tumor and sent it to pathology for more research. Cancer tumors have a grade of 1 through 3. Grade 1 is low-grade, well-differentiated cells. Grade 2 is moderately differentiated cells. The tumors in my body are grade 3, high-grade, poorly differentiated cells. Grade 3 cells are the most aggressive and dangerous cells threatening my body and my life.

Cancer is either hereditary and genetic, which means cancer genes were passed down from your parents, or environmental. Environmental cancer means your body was exposed to toxins from the outside world. Based on genetic testing and the biopsy that was taken for my body, the cancer inside me is 100 percent environmental. Over the last five years, I ate something or drank something that was highly toxic. These toxins caused cancer to grow in my digestive system.

Mucinous carcinoma of the abdomen is so rare that it only occurs in one in 2 million people. Let me say that again, the cancer inside me only affects one in 2 million people. My long-term survival rate is not good.

When you hear such devastating news, your mind explodes with emotions. This makes me sad. How did this happen? I am so angry because I take care of myself with exercise and I eat right with daily fruits and vegetables. I don't drink, I don't smoke, and I try to live life as a good person. Am I going to die? I must take care of my family. I can't die and leave my family. I can't leave my friends. I have a business with customers and coworkers who need me. I don't want to be sick and weak. *Why me? Why me? Why me?* I am just going to hide away where no one can see me and no one will find out that I have cancer.

If you are sick and depressed or just lost in a world of bad decisions, are you lonely, sad, or angry? I have been there. Darkness will enter your mind and try to destroy you. I have been there. Darkness feeds off your vulnerability and your weakness. I have been there. These dark forces take over your mind and try to destroy you. If you are sick and afraid, turn away from darkness.

Seek the light of the world. Always search for the light. Darkness in our world can destroy your life. So find the light of hope for tomorrow. Take control of your mind, and stay positive. A positive mental attitude will carry you past the darkness. Seek the light every day and *always* search for the light of hope for tomorrow.

My hope for tomorrow is that I will grow old with my wife, Beth. My hope is that my three sons fall in love and get married to a partner for life. My hope is to hold my grandbaby. My hope is to have celebrations with family and friends. My hope is to make a difference in this world. I want to bring happiness and love to all that I see. I love you all, and you have lifted my spirit. I have peace in my mind and hope in my heart.

Mucinous carcinoma cancer, guess what! I am going to beat you.

Stage 4 cancer means my doctors are on the offense and these harsh chemicals, chemotherapy, and surgery are going to destroy the cancer.

I am not afraid of grade 3 tumors!

Guess what. The cancer inside me is not hereditary so I can't pass on bad cancer cells to my sons Will, Thomas, and Miles. That is wonderful. So good and thankful.

Finally, I have a rare cancer, one in 2 million people. I will take those odds, and I am going to win! I am a unique man being one in 2 million people.

I am going to beat cancer with the light of the world, a positive attitude, and a love for life.

Do you know the light of the world? His name is Jesus Christ. Thank you for helping me. I love you all.

Cancer treatment with chemotherapy drugs made Bill sick with many bad side effects.

RING THE BELL AGAINST CANCER

Hi. This is Bill. I wanted to give you an update on my cancer treatments because today is the best day ever. I am at the cancer treatment infusion center and today will be my last day of chemotherapy. A lot has been happening and last week my doctors ordered an MRI. So far, I've had eleven chemotherapy infusions here at the treatment center. The MRI results created a great deal of concern from my doctors because the tumors in my abdomen are not shrinking. Under normal circumstances, chemotherapy drugs will stop or slow down the growth of tumors in your body. The MRI actually showed that one of the tumors in my body is growing more rapidly than ever before.

The chemotherapy drugs that are injected into my bloodstream are killing cancer cells and good cells as the chemicals move through my body. This terrible cancer in my body called mucinous carcinoma is not connected to my bloodstream. This cancerous mucus is floating in my abdomen and can't be reached by the chemotherapy drugs. This is a terrible discovery because the mucus is feeding the tumors with new cancer cells and uncontrollable growth. There is a battle going on in my body, and it has reached a stalemate. The chemotherapy drugs in my bloodstream are trying to destroy the tumors, and the mucus is feeding the tumors and giving them life.

My doctors are very concerned with this new development. Emory University Hospital is a research hospital so doctors collaborate to find solutions for medical issues. A large group of doctors joined together in the group is called the tumor board. Very rare, unusual, and life-threatening cancer cases are brought before the group of highly skilled doctors. My case was selected for review by the tumor board. After reviewing my case, the fourteen doctors who serve on the tumor board decided unanimously to stop my chemotherapy treatments.

The doctors agreed that surgery is the only lifesaving option for me. With surgery, doctors can open my abdomen to remove the mucus and cut away the cancerous tumors. Chemotherapy drugs will be poured directly into my abdomen to kill the remaining mucus and tumors. When I was originally diagnosed, I asked the doctor if he would go ahead and perform surgery. He said no because the traditional cancer protocol is to start with chemotherapy. I was very happy that the doctors agreed to move forward with surgery but very disappointed that they waited so long to make this decision. The many months of chemotherapy infusions into my body were devastating. The side effects from this poison made me sick and no doubt will have long-term effects on my body.

I believe the chemotherapy protocol process is an easy decision for the doctors to treat all cancer patients the same. All cancer is not the same, and this practice of treating all patients with chemotherapy should be reviewed by the doctors on an individual basis to determine its effectiveness. I also believe that hospitals and cancer treatment centers are businesses that need to make money and stay profitable. The hospital charged my insurance company $25,000 for each chemotherapy treatment. I received treatment for many months so you can see the economic benefit of chemotherapy for the hospital. A surprising 1.8 million Americans are diagnosed with cancer every year, so you can see treating cancer with chemotherapy has become an enormous moneymaking medical machine.

My body is very weak from the chemotherapy chemicals so I will need to wait six weeks before surgery. Chemo destroys the immune system in your body so surgery now would be too risky and life-threatening. This is a happy day for me because this chapter in my battle against cancer is over. No more nausea, fatigue, fever, diarrhea, rashes, hair loss, neuropathy, blood clots, internal bleeding, and other side effects caused by chemotherapy. The infusion PICC line has been removed, and I'm free from the pumps and poison that was injected into my body.

I am free, I am free, I am free! This is a celebration for life and good days ahead, feeling good, and just being normal without sickness or pain. As part of the celebration, my incredible wife, Beth, made me a poster to mark my last day at the chemotherapy infusion center. The poster said, "My last day of chemo is finally here! It makes me so happy I'm going to cheer! So let's ring this bell and run!"

Most chemotherapy infusion centers have a tradition of ringing a bell on your last day of treatment. Ringing the bell is a signal to all that you have graduated from this treatment process successfully with the help of compassionate nurses and a helpful medical team. The bell ringing is also a signal to the other cancer patients so they will be encouraged to continue on and cross the finish line of chemotherapy treatment.

Ring this bell, three times well; it is a toll to clearly say, "My treatment is done, this course is run, and I am on my way."

Let's get out of here!

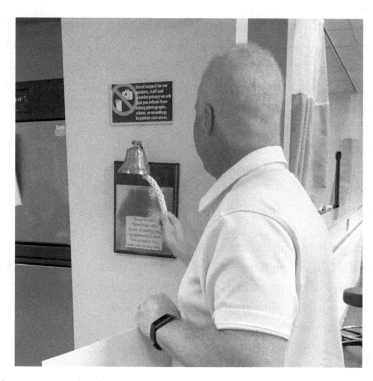

After many months of chemotherapy treatments to slow the spread of cancer, Bill rings the celebration bell as he leaves the infusion center on his final day.

FAILED CANCER SURGERY

Hi, everyone. This is Bill. I hope you're doing well. I wanted to give you an update on my battle with cancer. I've reached the most important point in this journey. Surgery and removing this cancer from my body. Next Wednesday, July 28, will be an important day in my life and my will to survive. Surgery is scheduled for Wednesday at Emory St. Joseph's Hospital in Sandy Springs, Georgia.

The surgery begins at 8:30 in the morning and lasts for fourteen hours. I met with my medical team on Friday before the surgery. The team consisted of three doctors, four nurses, and one anesthesiologist. The doctors and medical team will rotate through the fourteen-hour surgery. They will make a sixteen-inch incision across my abdomen. They will remove the three tumors visible on the MRI scan. They anticipate there will be smaller tumors to remove that were not detected in a scan. The small tumors are white and black spots and easy to see. The cancer in my body is so rare because of this deadly mucus that is floating around my abdomen. The mucus is cancer and spreads the tumors throughout my body. The doctors will spend most of their time removing this mucus, which is like jelly that builds up on my vital organs. My liver, stomach, kidneys, bladder, pancreas, spleen, and intestines are all covered with this cancerous mucus. They must scrape and scoop mucus from all these organs. It is impossible to remove all the mucus by hand. To kill the remaining hidden mucus, the doctors will pour chemotherapy chemicals directly into my open abdomen. Cancer cells are destroyed by heat. The chemotherapy chemical poison will be 110 degrees Fahrenheit. This hot, liquid poison will remain in my body for two hours. This part of the surgery is call hyperthermic intraperitoneal chemotherapy (HIPEC). This hot chemotherapy poison will kill any remaining cancer cells. This is the most important procedure because we must kill all the cancerous mucus for the cancer would just come back in my body over time.

The doctors will sew me up, and I will wake up sometime the next morning. I will be in the hospital for fourteen days to recover from the surgery. I will then return home to recover during August and September. This journey has been very long and difficult, but now I can see an end to my physical and mental pain.

Cancer is such a devastating disease, and I have experienced every human emotion during this journey. The fear of cancer, the fear of death, and now the fear of surgery are constantly in my mind.

I have been angry and mad about why this happened to me. Sadness is a heartbreaking emotion I experienced most days. The sadness of losing life and all that the wonderful world gives us.

But the most powerful and overwhelming emotion I experience every day is love. Love overcomes all and lifts my spirit with hope and happiness. Faith, hope, and love are all we need, and the greatest of these is love. My mind and heart are filled with peace and love. I have faith in God and the skills and talent of my medical team.

Life is a struggle between good and evil, right and wrong, and good health and bad health. We try to do what is good, but your mind and body enjoy bad things. What a terrible predicament you're in. Who will set you free from what is bad in your life?

Thank God! It has been done by Jesus Christ, our Savior! He has set us free!

I will win the battle against cancer, and I will be free.

Music is a great joy in my life, and I love all music. Here is my playlist I listen to every day:

- "What a Wonderful World" by Louis Armstrong
- "Dream On" by Aerosmith
- "Paint It Blue" by Charlie Crockett
- "Mister Blue Sky" by Electric Light Orchestra
- "I Believe" by Chilliwack
- "The Old Rugged Cross" by Alan Jackson
- "Amazing Grace" by Carrie Underwood
- "Victory in Jesus" by Alan Jackson
- "Somewhere over the Rainbow" by the Ukulele boys

Music plays an important role in my battle against cancer. I hope you can use music and songs to calm your soul and give you peace and understanding through the journey of life.

Bill in the hospital after cancer surgery.

HOME FROM THE HOSPITAL

Hello, everyone. I hope you're doing well. I'm home from the hospital. I convinced my doctor to let me go because my pain level was at 5 out of 10. My body is still in bad shape from surgery, and I look like Frankenstein because the incision in my abdomen is sixteen inches long. I have forty-six staples across my abdomen, and after a lot of pain and infection in this area, it was determined that I was allergic to titanium staples. The staples were removed and the healing process will take several months.

I have had a tube down my throat for several days because of surgery complications. My stomach and intestines were in shock from the surgery and failed to work. After several days of medication and movement, my stomach and intestines woke up and are now working. The tube down my throat affected my voice so I was unable to talk for a few days. When I'm able to talk again, I have very disappointing news to share with you.

Hi, everyone. This is Bill. I wanted to give you an update on my battle with cancer. I had surgery last month, and shortly after my doctor came into my room, he held my hand and said, "Bill, I'm sorry. The surgery failed. Cancer has spread to your liver, and it can't be removed. You have no other options for surgery. You have stage 4 cancer, and you have a 20 percent chance to live for five years." The doctor also said he could put me back on chemotherapy for the rest of my life, but he did not know if the chemotherapy worked.

Stop for a moment. A doctor just told me that I was going to die within five years. My mind was overwhelmed with shock and sadness. How could this happen, why did this happen, and how can this happen to me?

Let's erase that bad news from our minds and focus on good news. That same doctor said, "Bill, God may have a different plan for you and you can live longer. We just don't know." I choose God's plan because God knows me better than anyone. God knows that after Him, my family is everything to me. God knows that I love life, I love freedom, and I love everyone because God is love.

God knows I will never give up on life and I will fight to live tirelessly every day. A long time ago, God planned for me to help cancer patients find a cure for cancer. My mission from God is clear, and I will never stop working to help those with cancer who feel they have no hope.

I am not giving up on a medical breakthrough for this rare cancer in my body. My family and friends have encouraged me to get a second opinion. A friend who is also a cancer patient gave me two great recommendations. On October 21, I will be traveling to Houston, Texas, and meeting with doctors at MD Anderson Cancer Center. This hospital is ranked as the top cancer treatment center in the United States. I am getting a third opinion from Stanford University Hospital in California. They review all your medical history and give an online review so there is no need to travel. The cancer in my body occurs in one in 2 million people. My hope is that these hospitals in other parts of our country will have helped people with my rare cancer.

A small miracle has already happened. All cancer patients get regular blood work. A tumor marker is cancer cells and good cells flowing through your body. Doctors review your blood work and look at a tumor marker scale. A scale of 1–5 means your cancer is not spreading. A scale of

12–20 means your cancer is aggressive and spreading rapidly. The scale of above 20 means cancer is all over your body.

Back in April, just after I was diagnosed with cancer, my tumor marker was 11. This means the cancer in my body was highly aggressive and ready to spread throughout my body.

Last Friday, my blood work showed my tumor marker at 1.3. From 11 in April to 1.3 in August after the surgery. That is a miracle. The surgery failed, but God's healing hand is destroying the cancer inside my body. Praise be to God, and blessed be the name of Jesus Christ.

Hi, everyone. I wanted to give you an update on my battle against cancer. Beth and I traveled to the University of Texas MD Anderson Cancer Center in Houston this week. We wanted to get a second opinion on my medical condition after my failed cancer surgery during the summer. I can tell you that Beth, my boys, and I have a new feeling of hope. The doctors were very positive and have a different plan.

This cancer inside me is extremely rare. It occurs in one out of every 2 million people. This medical team at MD Anderson Cancer Center has treated 1,600 patients with the same rare cancer as me. I feel that experience will be helpful to me. The new doctors took scans of my body and saw a cancer tumor on the ligament of my liver that is different from my prior diagnosis. The new doctors see my cancer cells as moderate and not aggressive. The cancer is only on my liver, no other organs. My liver is functioning normally. The new doctors want to do arthroscopic surgery to see the tumor directly. They are also open to trying the HIPEC surgery again.

Here is the great news. This cancer inside me is not growing. The new doctors said the cancer has not changed in the last three months. Jesus, the great physician, is performing a miracle inside my body.

The doctors ordered two different tumor marker blood tests. The normal tumor marker in the first test is 35. My score was 36.7. The normal tumor marker in the second test is a range of 1–5. My score was 2.2.

The new doctors gave me a very different opinion on chemotherapy. They said, "You don't need chemotherapy if your cancer is not growing." They determined the best course of action would be to monitor my blood work and do periodic CT scans. They would only add chemotherapy drugs to my treatment when and if it was needed.

My family and I have decided to move forward with this positive and hopeful new plan. Getting a second opinion was one of the most important decisions I have ever made in my life. I am traveling back to Houston next month to continue the process.

I've always tried to take care of myself by eating right, exercising, and taking care of my body. This is more important than ever now, and I am going to do everything I can do mentally and physically to stay strong and positive.

My faith has become the most important tool I have to fight cancer. I read passages from the Bible every day to use the Word of God to heal my body. Here are some of God's words I use to heal my body:

My God in heaven, hear my prayer and heal my body.

> At one time you were separated from God. You were enemies in your minds because of your evil ways. But because Christ died, God has brought you back to himself. Christ's death has made you holy in God's sight. So now you don't have any flaw. You are free from blame. (Colossians 1:21–22 NIRV)

My God in heaven, hear my prayer and heal my body.

> God gave the command and healed them, so they were saved from dying. (Psalm 107:20 NCV)

My God in heaven, hear my prayer and heal my body.

> Therefore, submit to God. Resist the devil and he will flee from you. (James 4:7 NKJV)

My God in heaven, hear my prayer and heal my body.

> I shall not die, but live, and declare the works of the Lord. (Psalm 118:17 KJV)

My God in heaven, hear my prayer and heal my body.

> Let all that I am praise the Lord; may I never forget the good things he does for me. He forgives all my sins and heals all my diseases. He redeems me from death and crowns me with love and tender mercies. He fills my life with good things. My youth is renewed like the eagle's! (Psalm 103:2–5 NLT)

My God in heaven, hear my prayer and heal my body.

> You must serve only the Lord your God. If you do, I will bless you with food and water, and I will protect you from illness. There will be no miscarriages or infertility in your land, and I will give you long, full lives. (Exodus 23:25–26 NLT)

Beth, Will, Thomas, Miles, and I are going to live one day at a time. We are going to cherish every moment of every day we have together on earth. We will have hope for tomorrow. At night we will dream for another day. We will dream on until all our dreams come true.

When cancer treatments and surgery failed, Bill never gave up on life. He stayed positive and got a second doctors opinion.

Cure cancer. It's a political decision!
Love life.
Love freedom.
Love everyone.
God is love.

- 10 million people in the world die from cancer every year.
- The total annual economic cost of cancer is estimated at $1.16 trillion.
- Cancer is the leading cause of death by disease in children.
- 600,000 Americans die from cancer each year.
- 1.8 million Americans are diagnosed with cancer each year.

Cancer is not from God. Cancer comes from the internal and environmental darkness of our world. God has had enough with cancer! No more death from cancer! God says we must cure cancer. God says there is a cure for cancer. But walls and barriers are stopping the discovery of a cure for cancer. Artificial walls and barriers must be removed. Political walls are stopping a cure for cancer. Money and its economic impact are stopping a cure for cancer. Global forces are stopping a cure for cancer. These artificial walls and barriers must be removed to cure cancer.

There is another message for the world to hear. God says there is evil and darkness covering the earth. Turn to God. Have faith in God and only God. The world is filled with anger and hatred. But God is the God of love and peace. Turn to God and away from evil and darkness. Love life, love freedom, and love everyone. God is love.

In the Bible, God gave the Israelites the Ark of the Covenant, which contained the Ten Commandments. Joshua used the ark to remove walls and barriers and open the Promised Land to the Israelites. Today, we have a new covenant that is represented by the cross and the blood of Jesus Christ. The cross and our faith will be used to remove walls and barriers so we can find a cure for cancer and renew our love for God.

In the Bible, Joshua 6:1–5 (NLT) says the following:

Now the gates of Jericho were tightly shut because the people were afraid of the Israelites. No one was allowed to go in or out.

But the Lord said to Joshua, I've given you Jericho, its king, and all its mighty warriors.

Your entire army is to march around the city once a day for six days.

Seven priests will walk ahead of the ark, each carrying a ram's horn. On the seventh day you are to march around the city seven times, with the priests blowing the horns.

When you hear the priest give one long blast on the horns, have all the people give a mighty shout. Then the walls of the city will collapse, and the people can charge straight into the town.

The ancient city of Jericho was surrounded by walls and barriers. God told Joshua and the Israelites to carry the Ark of the Covenant around Jericho seven times. God told Joshua and the Israelites to give one long sound on a ram's horn. God told Joshua and the Israelites to give a mighty shout. God gave Jericho to Joshua and the Israelites. The walls and barriers were removed by God.

Joshua 1:9 (NLT) says, "God said to Joshua and God has said to me. This is my command—be strong and courageous! Do not be afraid or discouraged. For the Lord your God is with you wherever you go."

Washington, DC, is the capital of the United States and the political foundation of our country. Political change starts in this city, and the decisions made by our elected officials can change the world. I believe that if we remove political walls and barriers, a cure for cancer will be found.

I am a man with stage 4 cancer, so God sent me to Washington, DC. God had two steps in my mission. The first step was a test of my faith. The second step was choosing a messenger who had been stricken by this terrible disease.

God tests our faith in many ways. Sometime the test is small, but some tests are so big that they become life-changing events.

One of the greatest tests of faith occurs in the Old Testament of the Bible. God sent Abraham and his only son, Isaac, to give a sacrifice. When they arrived at the sacrificial altar, God instructed Abraham to sacrifice Isaac. This was a test of Abraham's faith to God. Just as Abraham was about to sacrifice his only son, God stopped him. Abraham's faith endured, and God instructed Abraham to sacrifice a ram instead of his son.

God tested my faith in a much different way on my mission to Washington, DC. I was instructed to carry a cross and two banners in our nation's capital. I was also instructed by God to use a shofar ram's horn made in Israel to deliver a mighty sound. The construction of the cross was to be eight feet tall and four feet wide, made with metal, and painted white. I contacted a steeple-making company in Alabama. We reached an agreement on the cost of the cross, and the company was ready to start production. The only issue that developed was the weight of the cross. I would be carrying the cross on my shoulder in Washington, DC, and a solid metal structure would be too heavy. The solution was to make the metal cross hollow inside, but with this modification the weight was still heavy at 42 pounds. I trained for the mission by walking long distances and carrying the cross on my shoulder. The two banners were much easier to produce. I contacted a local sign company and purchased two freestanding banners that were easy to transport. My instruction for the banners was clear. The message from God on the first banner was "Cure cancer. It's a political decision." The message for the second banner was "Love Life, Love Freedom, Love Everyone, God is love." I contacted a business in Israel and purchased a shofar ram's horn. I practiced using the horn in my home, and the Holy Spirit inside me delivered the sound of God.

I live in Atlanta, Georgia, so the journey to Washington, DC, required a lot of preparation. The political environment in our country is volatile, and although we live in a free country, you can't just march on Washington. Any event or demonstration near the White House, the United States Capitol, or the US Supreme Court requires a permit.

The secret service guards the White House so I called the Washington, DC, secret service office to get permission for my event. I told the secret service agent that I would be carrying a cross in front of the White House seven times. I told him I would display the two banners in front of the White House and I would give a mighty sound using a ram's horn. The secret service agent said my cause was noble and I was free to carry out my demonstration.

The Capitol building is guarded by the United States Capitol Police. Events that take place around the Capitol require permits. This permit process required filling out a written document and answering many questions that related to the event. There were many guidelines and restrictions in place, and after many weeks of waiting, I was given the official approval permit on the day of my event. I could carry the cross, display the banners, and sound the ram's horn in front of the United States Capitol.

The United States Supreme Court security has the most restrictive guidelines for events and demonstrations. I told Supreme Court security that I wanted to carry a cross in front of the building seven times, display two banners, and use a ram's horn. All three were denied. I was given permission by the Supreme Court security to make a loud statement at a specified location in front of the building. So I decided to buy a blow horn that would carry a sound two hundred times louder than my normal voice.

The United States Park Service controls security in all of the general areas around the monuments in Washington, DC. My greatest fear in preparation for this journey was being arrested and jailed for displaying my faith. I thought about Paul and Peter in the Bible and all the times they were arrested for demonstrating their faith and spreading the Word of God. The United States Park

Service officer told me my demonstration was a very noble cause and assured me that I would not be arrested.

My wife and sons joined me on this road trip to Washington. We loaded the eight-foot cross, the two large banners, and the shofar ram's horn in the back of my son's Ford F150 truck. We all loaded in the truck and set off on the two-day road trip to carry out my mission.

Washington, DC, is a large city so I made hotel reservations in two locations: one near the White House and the other close to the United States Capitol and Supreme Court building. As we checked into one, the hotel's the staff was very surprised by the eight-foot cross that we carried to our room. I just smiled and told them we were a part of a peaceful demonstration.

Our plan for the peaceful demonstration was simple and would take three days. On Tuesday I would carry the cross in front of the White House. The banners would be erected to stand in front of the White House, and I would sound the ram's horn when I finished walking in front of the White House seven times. On Wednesday I would carry the cross in front of the United States Capitol seven times. The banners would be displayed in front of the Capitol, and I would sound the ram's horn. On Thursday I would go to the designated area in front of the Supreme Court and proclaim God's message with the blow horn.

I was very nervous on Tuesday morning when I woke up, anticipating the uncertainty of what might happen during this event in front of the White House. I pray daily, but this morning, I prayed especially hard for the strength to carry out my mission and God's protection for my family.

We decided to leave and walk to the White House at 11 a.m. so we would catch the lunch crowd around this busy time of day. A miracle from God occurred on that morning. As you know, I had stage 4 cancer with a 20 percent chance to live for five years. Little did I know that over a thousand miles away from me in Houston, Texas, a group of doctors at MD Anderson Cancer Center was reviewing my medical case. God intervened for me that morning and opened the minds and talents of those doctors to save my life. With unanimous decisions, the doctors agreed that they could successfully perform surgery on me and remove the cancer that would save my life.

At 10:30 a.m., just thirty minutes before my family and I would leave for the White House, my cell phone rang. I answered the phone, and the medical team from MD Anderson Cancer Center told me they had good news. Surgery would save my life, and they were willing to help me.

God tested my faith. The long journey to Washington, DC, and the meticulous planning for the event was a test of my faith. Just before I carried out my mission from God, He rewarded me with life. I followed God's Word, and He used the doctors' God-given talents and surgical skills to help me remove the cancer from my body. I graciously thanked the doctors and made plans to travel to Houston in the coming weeks. When I hung up from the phone call, I was overwhelmed with joy and hope for my future with my family. The Holy Spirit filled my heart with joy.

My family and I made the two-block walk to the White House. The president was at the White House that day, signing the infrastructure bill into law. The weather was beautiful on that day, and the sun was shining brightly directly over the White House. On most days in our democratic republic, you will find many groups protesting and demonstrating outside the White House. The freedom to assemble and the freedom of speech are the foundation of our republic. God opened the stage for me in front of the White House that day, and I was the only one demonstrating. No other groups were around to distract from my message.

I carried the cross in front of the White House seven times. Then I use the shofar ram's horn to play a mighty sound. I finished the event with a mighty shout. "Cure cancer! It's a political decision. Love life, love freedom, love everyone, God is love." There were many people present that day to hear God's message. The Holy Spirit was responsible for carrying the message to the president of the United States inside the White House.

On Wednesday morning, my family and I left the new hotel and walked to the front of the United States Capitol building. Once again, the day was beautiful with no clouds in the sky. The sun was shining brightly, and God's presence was all around us. I carried the cross in front of the Capitol seven times. I played the ram's horn with a loud sound. I gave a mighty shout for all to hear. "Love life, love freedom, love everyone, God is love. Cure cancer! It's a political decision!"

Thursday was our final day in Washington, DC. The final day of my mission from God. My family and I walked to the Supreme Court building. I confirmed with the Supreme Court security officer to make sure I was in the proper place to deliver my message. The Supreme Court justices were present that day in the building, and I used my mega blow horn so they could hear my voice. The megaphone was two hundred times more powerful than my human voice. There is no doubt my message was heard.

I said, "Love life, love freedom, love everyone, God is love. Six hundred thousand Americans die from cancer each year, and 1.8 million Americans are diagnosed with cancer each year. Cancer is not from God. Cancer comes from the internal environmental darkness of our world. God has had enough with cancer! No more death from cancer! God says we must cure cancer. God says there is a cure for cancer. But walls and barriers are stopping the discovery of a cure for cancer. Artificial walls and barriers must be removed. Political walls are stopping a cure for cancer. Money and its economic impact are stopping a cure for cancer. Global forces are stopping a cure for cancer. These artificial walls and barriers must be removed to cure cancer. God says there are evil and darkness covering the earth. We must turn to God and away from evil and darkness. We must have faith in God and only God. The world is filled with anger and hatred. But God is the God of love and peace. Turn to God and away from evil and darkness. Love life, love freedom, love everyone, God is love."

The ancient Israelites used the Ark of the Covenant to break down walls and barriers and open the Promised Land. I used the new covenant, which is represented by the cross and the blood of Jesus Christ. The cross and my faith were used to remove walls and barriers so we can find a cure for cancer and renew our love for God. I used the shofar ram's horn and made a mighty sound so all the people in Washington, DC, could hear the sound of God. Like the ancient Israelites, I gave a mighty shout and proclaimed that we must turn away from the darkness of sin and destruction and place our complete faith in God.

God will save us all.

My family and I returned to Georgia with a sense of peace for today and hope for tomorrow. God's mighty power will be used to change the hearts and minds of those in political power now and in the future. I am a sinful man saved by grace and tested for my faith. My faith is strong because I know God's love for me will endure forever.

Bill at the White House demonstration.

Bill carrying the cross in front of the White House.

Bill delivering God's message at United States Capitol in Washington, D.C.

Bill carrying the cross at the United States Capitol.

Bill speaking God's word at the Supreme Court.

JANUARY 11 AND HOPE

Hi, everyone. This is Bill. I hope you had a Merry Christmas and a happy New Year. Next Tuesday, January 11, I will have surgery to remove the cancer in my body. After getting a second opinion from the doctors at MD Anderson Cancer Center in Houston, my new doctors have decided that surgery is the best option for me.

Three surgeons in Houston reviewed the surgery notes from Emory Hospital in Atlanta about the failed operation I had last summer. They also completed their own MRI and CT scans of my body. The new doctors disagree with the surgery notes from Emory. The Emory surgeon said the cancer tumors in my body were as hard as cement. He could not remove the tumors so he had to abort the process and end the operation. His medical mission failed.

The new Houston doctors have operated on many patients with this rare cancer inside me. They have never seen or encountered tumors like cement or concrete. So on Tuesday morning, the doctors will begin with laparoscopic surgery. With small incisions, they will place a camera in my abdomen to look at the cancer tumors. If the tumors are like cement, the surgery will end. If this happens, there are no more medical options for me. I pray that the surgeons see something different. I pray that they can remove the tumors and set me free from cancer.

A doctor will make a sixteen-inch incision across my abdomen and cut the tumors out. The HIPEC surgery process will then put hot chemotherapy liquid in the open area of my abdomen for two hours. This will destroy other cancer cells with direct contact. He will sew me up, and I will recover in the hospital. Medical reports say that if the surgery is successful, I have an 82 percent chance to survive for five years. I feel good today. I have no pain in my body. My mind and body are ready to be cancer free forever. Thank you for your prayers and encouragement. God is in control of my life. I love you all.

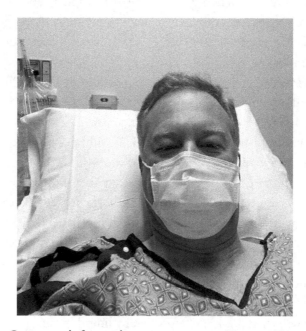

Getting ready for another cancer surgery in Houston, Texas.

Hey, everybody. It's Bill.

We have beat cancer. We have beat cancer. We have beat cancer.

The most important thing for someone facing cancer or any kind of sickness is having a support group. I can't tell you enough how much I appreciate all of you who have prayed for me, who have sent me texts, who have sent me cards, who have sent me flowers, who have sent me T-shirts, who have sent me books—whatever it may be. Thank you, thank you, thank you, because together we have beat cancer.

I want to thank the amazing team at MD Anderson Cancer Center in Houston. I have been in the hospital for twenty-eight days. Let me repeat that. I have been in the hospital for twenty-eight days. I want to thank my physician. Dr. Paul Mansfield took my medical case, and I asked him why he took my case. "There are millions of people with cancer in the world. Why did you choose me to help with my medical condition?" He said, "Bill your cancer is so rare and it occurs in only one in 2 million people. We were connected. You found me, and I found you."

Dr. Mansfield removed forty-nine small tumors from my abdomen during sixteen hours of surgery. The medical team then performed the HIPEC surgery whereby they flushed and washed my entire abdomen with hot chemotherapy chemicals that were 110 degrees Fahrenheit. This part of the surgery lasted for two hours, and the nurses refer to it as shake and bake because they move my body back and forth as the hot chemotherapy drug moves through all areas of my abdomen to kill any remaining cancer cells.

The surgery was very successful, and Dr. Mansfield's entire medical team was amazing during these sixteen hours of surgery to save my life. I was then moved to the hospital to start my recovery. The hospital nurses and other medical personnel have all been absolutely incredible. I did face some challenges, because I was scheduled to be released a long time ago. Things just did not work out as I had hoped they would, and shortly after the surgery, I could not eat for eight days. My entire abdomen had shut down and gone to sleep so I had no bowel movement. Finally, after eight days of no food, I was able to eat some broth and Jell-O. To make matters worse, I then contracted an infection. The doctors inserted 4 JP drain tubes in my body during surgery to remove liquid waste. In the area around the tubes, I contracted a staph infection. It took several weeks to get the infection under control with antibiotics. We then faced two other obstacles during recovery. The vagus nerve that crosses the stomach was damaged during surgery and caused severe pain for me every time I tried to eat. I was also diagnosed with gastroparesis and the doctors are trying to resolve this issue with medication. This medication enables my stomach to wake up because it also shut down during surgery and food was unable to move through my body.

Everything I'm telling you is a miracle. Truly a miracle. Think about what has happened. Six months ago, I was sent home to die. My medical condition was considered so bad by the old doctors that I was sent home to die. Here I am today, an absolute miracle. I praise God and thank you because faith and a positive attitude carried me through this difficult time. I never gave up, even during the most difficult pain and hardship. Several days my temperature was over 103 degrees Fahrenheit because of the infection in my body. The nurses placed ice over my body to cool me down, lower my temperature, and keep me from overheating. There were difficulties, but I never lost my faith.

I never lost my faith.

So anybody who is facing adversity, never give up, keep your faith, and keep your love. You should always know that love surpasses all. We can come together and help each other.

Now I'm going to tell the world about this miracle that happened to me by the grace of God. Cancer is a devastating disease for everybody, but together we can overcome it and win the battle. With faith in our great healer, Jesus Christ, and a positive attitude, we can come together for good. By His stripes, we are healed, and I will not die but live and proclaim the works of God.

After twenty-eight days in this hospital room, my hope and faith are as strong as they have ever been. I am saved, I am happy, and I love you all. Godspeed to everyone.

After surgery Bill spent 28 days in the hospital and 47 days in Houston during recovery.
He finally returned home to Georgia celebrated by his family and friends.

On January 11, 2022, I underwent cancer surgery at MD Anderson Cancer Center in Houston. The day began for me at 3:30 a.m. when I awoke to shower and get ready in the hotel room. Beth, Thomas, and Miles were fast asleep as we had watched the national college football championship the night before. Georgia and Alabama had a gridiron battle on the playing field. The University of Georgia won and became the national champion for the first time in forty years. We celebrated in the hotel room until midnight. With big hugs and a few tears, I said bye to Thomas and Miles at 4:30 a.m. Beth and I then walked across the street to MD Anderson Hospital for a 5 a.m. surgery check-in. The day before, Monday, January 10, had been busy with preoperation doctors' appointments and the all-important COVID-19 test that must be negative to have surgery. The doctors were also tested and everyone had negative results, so surgery could proceed.

When we arrived at the hospital check-in, a lady standing in front of us was informed she tested positive for COVID-19 the day before, so her surgery was postponed. It surprised and shocked Beth and me. We also worried this contagious disease might infect us. The hospital staff escorted the lady away, and we moved on to the surgery waiting room.

A team of doctors and nurses came into the room to review procedures and prepare me for surgery. It was about 6 a.m. The last group of doctors to visit me was the anesthesiologist. Little did I know that the surgery would last for sixteen hours. I kissed Beth and gave her all my love as we shared a few tears.

The anesthesia was administered and I began to fall asleep. As the medical team of about eight people rolled me down the hall, I held Beth's hand. Suddenly, I sat straight up in the bed and yelled, "Wait! Wait! Wait! Please stop." The medical team was alarmed and stopped rolling the bed. The doctor said, "What do you need, Mr. Hembree?" I said, "We can't go on. We must wait. A priest is coming to pray with me." The medical team looked at Beth, and she smiled. She said, "A priest is Catholic, and we are not Catholic. Bill must be dreaming."

They continued on to the operating room. It was 7 a.m., Tuesday, January 11, 2022. The surgery to remove cancer for my body had begun.

For the next sixteen hours, many miracles happened to me, and I want to share this miraculous journey with you. As I lay on the operating table, a sixteen-inch incision opened my abdomen so that cancerous tumors could be removed. Forty-nine tumors that looked like glue were cut from many organs, including the largest on my liver. Hour after hour passed as the surgeon meticulously removed all those glue-like cancer tumors from my body. Hot chemotherapy chemicals at 110 degrees Fahrenheit were poured into my abdomen to wash and flush small cancer cells out of my body.

During this absolute trauma to my body, a miracle occurred.

While my body lay on that operating table in Houston, my spirit and soul left the earth. There was no tunnel with light at the end, and there was no floating in the hospital room above my body. The most incredible event of my life happened. It was so amazing that it takes my breath away to think about it now. With God as my witness, I make this proclamation to you. I woke up at the gates of heaven holding the right hand of Jesus Christ. My spirit and soul are overwhelmed with wonderful emotions as I tell you what happened to me.

Jesus was radiant. His elegance and glory were the most beautiful things I have ever seen. Jesus was so handsome, and His smile warmed my heart. There was light all around me, and Jesus led me forward. His comforting presence gave me peace and happiness. I had no fear because He was with me. As we left the gates, I could see the kingdom of heaven above us on the top of the hill. A white marble road was shining and open for us to walk along. Rolling hills rose up from the pathway. Angels stood on the hills around us. Thousands of angels proclaimed the glory of God and celebrated the presence of Jesus. My name was announced, and there was a mighty shout of victory from the multitude of angels. Jesus held my hands tightly and looked at me with joy and happiness. Music, beautiful music, was playing all around us. As we walked closer and closer to the kingdom of heaven, the jubilation and celebration of the angels grew louder and stronger. This was a celebration for eternal life and victory over darkness.

I was overwhelmed with emotions at the center of this heavenly domain. My faith in Jesus and the grace of God delivered my salvation. It was a victory for me on being a good and faithful servant. I stood with Jesus as the parade of angels and the concert of music surrounded me. The atmosphere was wonderful. The glory of God was around us as we marched forward in celebration. I was in paradise. The beauty from the sound of God and the light of God was pure love and perfection.

We entered the kingdom of heaven, and it was a city with streets of gold and mansions. I saw the faces of people everywhere. Everyone was busy and working to glorify God. There were children everywhere. So many children. And the people were filled with love and joy in the presence of Jesus.

Jesus took me to a beautiful mansion made of sandstone with large columns in front. We walked inside, and there was a beautiful courtyard with flowers and fountains flowing with crystal water. There was a large auditorium inside the mansion. People were working and getting ready to worship God. Everyone had a purpose and a responsibility in heaven. There was complete satisfaction in every job as I saw joy and happiness with all the people. There was no sense of time in heaven. Time didn't exist.

Jesus took me to three churches in heaven: a large church, a medium church, and a small church. There was always beautiful music playing everywhere. There was music inside the churches and outside in the city. Each church had a grand service. The people sang and rejoiced as they worshiped God. They joined together in each church and gave praise to God with everlasting love. There were people taking care of children in each church. Everyone was moving and busy with what they were doing at the churches.

Jesus took me out of the city in heaven. Heaven is also filled with a beautiful countryside. Rolling hills and flat, grassy plains were all around us. There were green pastures and still waters. Flowers and orchards were all around us. It was the Garden of Eden. It was quiet and peaceful. There were no mansions in this heavenly place. Just paradise everywhere I looked. It was absolutely beautiful.

Then Jesus took me to the Crystal Sea. This part of heaven was a coastline that bordered the sparkling waters of the Crystal Sea. The shining water spread out from the land with dazzling color. The beach was covered in soft, white sand. The sand dunes rolled along the coastline, and there was a cool breeze. The water was calm and the waves were gentle as they crashed along the shore. The air was fresh, and the sound was peaceful. The light of God shown all around us. The sea was endless as it spread out in front of me. As I turned around, I could see mountains rising up from the sea. From the beach, I could see mansions all along the coast. The mansions here were different from the city.

Jesus took me to a mansion above the beach. It did not have columns and was low on the hillside. It was made of white marble and spread out over the land. The roof and walls had sharp lines and *many* rooms. Balconies overlooked the Crystal Sea. The views were stunningly beautiful. There were many people inside this marble mansion. They were greeting each other, laughing, singing, and praising God. Again, there was wonderful music everywhere. The music was so pleasing to me. In each room, we saw people in small groups joining together with celebrations. As I stood there looking at the beauty of paradise around me, the glory of God filled my spirit. Jesus was always with me, holding my hand and guiding me through heaven.

Suddenly, the mansion on the Crystal Sea was gone. Once again, I was standing with Jesus at the gates of heaven. He smiled at me, touched my face, and told me He loved me. Jesus is pure love. He comforted me and reassured me of His everlasting love. He reminded me that He was with me always and carried me in times of trouble. He told me that I did not see all of the kingdom of heaven because this was not my time. He said, "Later, you will have a big role to play in heaven. You will see the face of God. You will see family and friends and be reunited together forever. You will spend eternity in paradise. But first, you have more work to do on earth." Jesus told me to heal the sick and tell the world what I saw in heaven.

Jesus kissed my head, and again the music began to play. I looked at His smiling face and the glowing radiance around Him. I felt pure love and joy and peace. The light of the world was shining on me in the kingdom of heaven. He said, "I will see you again," and released my hand.

The light of heaven was gone. The music and the beautiful sounds of heaven stopped.

I opened my eyes again. I was in a dimly lit hospital room. Light from the hallway entered the room. A nurse stood over me as I woke up. I asked her, "Are we in heaven?" She said, "No, you are recovering from surgery in the hospital." I asked her if she heard the music. She said no. She said I had been in surgery for sixteen hours. The doctors had removed forty-nine cancerous tumors from my body. She said the surgery was successful.

I smiled and held my thoughts to myself. My heart was filled with love and peace. For sixteen hours, Jesus opened my eyes and carried me to the kingdom of heaven. My commission, my instruction, my duty, and my command are to share this good news with the world.

CANCER STRIKES AGAIN

The terrible reality about cancer is that it keeps coming back. Most cancer patients are on a five-year observation plan. CT scans, PET scans, MRIs, and bloodwork are completed every three months, six months, and yearly. Most doctors believe that if your scans are clear for five years, you can carry the designation of being cancer free. Even though cancer patients may have a successful surgery, many rounds of chemotherapy, and radiation treatments, tiny cancer cells can be hidden in their bodies. These tiny cells will join to create new tumors. These new tumors can attack your body's vital organs and threaten your life. This vicious cycle can start over again. It is a constant physical and mental battle that we must deal with every day. There is so much anxiety and concern as we prepare for the next checkup. Will the scans be clear, and will we be able to carry on with a normal healthy life? Or will cancer strike again and require us to get more medical treatments and live with a dark cloud of uncertainty about our future?

I have found several ways to deal with this challenge. The three most important actions I pursue to help my mind and body are prayer, faith, and peace. I pray my regular prayers in the morning and at night. I have a list of family and friends that I pray for. I have a list of people with cancer and other sicknesses that I pray for. I pray for our country and our state. I pray that our national and state leaders will make decisions that are guided by Judeo-Christian principles. I read Bible verses every day and review a list of my favorites. I have three daily devotional books that have encouraging words and help me in my daily Christian walk. I read the Word of God and speak the Word of God out loud. I use my voice to proclaim the awesome power and everlasting love of our Father in heaven. I use passages from the Bible, which is the Word of God, to heal my body. I am healed and made whole by the Word of God.

Throughout my day, I talk to Jesus. I offer short prayers in my mind. These small prayers help me to stay in constant contact with Jesus. I seek wisdom, guidance, and help from Jesus as I make daily decisions. I may hear a story about a person in need and say a short prayer to Jesus. I constantly pray for my family and ask Jesus to bless them and protect them, give them wisdom and common sense, and keep them healthy and strong. I ask Jesus to help me be more faithful. I sometimes struggle with my faith throughout the day. My sickness sometimes causes pain and I ask Jesus to heal my pain. Some days I get trapped in the world of self-pity and ask Jesus to clear my mind. I try to think of positive thoughts. The sinful world around us is filled with temptations and evil. On a day when my mind is filled with temptation, I say a short prayer to Jesus and ask Him to deliver me from evil. My faith is not strong enough because I am a weak human being who struggles with daily sin. Even though I love God's laws, my mind is held captive to the sinful nature inside me. No matter how hard I try to do what is right, I constantly make bad decisions. Jesus is the only way to free yourself from sin. My little talks with Jesus throughout the day give me peace, hope, and freedom to overcome any challenge that stands before me.

If we release our troubles and place them in the hands of Jesus, our minds and bodies will be free. You will find peace because Jesus will take care of your worldly trials and tribulations. Jesus is with us during every step we take throughout our journeys in life. He always holds our hand and sometimes carries us through difficulties. But be assured that Jesus will never abandon you or forsake you. His love endures forever. Talk to Jesus throughout your day, and listen for His voice. His voice and direction will give you a peaceful life if you follow Him. There are so many voices in this world that try to control our minds. You will never find peace if you listen to the voices of this world. These bad voices cause stress. Stress will consume your mind and body and destroy you. Stress is a leading cause of sickness. Mental and physical stress plague our lives. I believe that stress that is caused by the internal and environmental darkness of our world causes cancer. Release yourself from this stressful captivity. Find peaceful daily meditation with Jesus. Constantly talk with Jesus throughout your day with short and meaningful prayers. Be thankful as you pray. We have so much to be grateful for in our daily lives. Jesus will give us all that we need, and we should thank Him for his love, protection, and guidance. Prayer is the foundation of the relationship with Jesus. Through prayer, you will find faith, and a growing faith will give you peace.

A strong spiritual life is critical in a fight against cancer or any sickness. Another very important factor in fighting cancer and staying healthy is eating the right food. The cancer inside me is not hereditary, so no member of my family passed these cancer genes to my body. The cancer inside me is 100 percent environmental. That means toxins in the food I consumed caused me to have cancer. This is a very frustrating fact because I have always tried to maintain a healthy diet. I believe cancer-causing agents are in our foods and drinks. Since I was diagnosed with cancer, my family has tried to change our eating habits. This is one of the most difficult challenges you will face. Eating healthy sounds easy, right? Think again. Fast food is all around us, and it is usually not good for our bodies. Our fast-paced world leads us to fast food. I have tried and tried to develop alternatives in my eating habits but have found it to be impossible to accomplish every day. I still eat fast food, but I have made a lot of improvements. Just do the best you can every day, and your body will appreciate the changes.

My wife, Beth, is the love of my life and the best cook I have ever known. She has done an excellent job at educating herself about harmful foods. All the food she prepares for our family is healthy. While she is grocery shopping, she closely reviews the ingredients of the food she purchases.

She always stays away from added sugar in food. She stays away from processed foods. She buys organic food. She avoids foods that are sprayed with the chemical glyphosate. We eat a lot of fruit and vegetables, and she has a thorough cleaning process to help eliminate any harmful pesticides. We eat grass-fed beef raised by local farmers. She also buys goods from the local farmers market. There is a saying "No farms, no food." We support the farming community and appreciate all the hard work farmers do every day to feed our world.

The first step I took toward better habits was drinking water with my meals. Just drink a glass of water with breakfast, lunch, and dinner. I love to drink a cup of coffee in the morning, and research has shown that coffee helps your liver. I still have an occasional soft drink, but I limit myself. I try to drink grapefruit juice, carrot juice, or celery juice every day. I like the taste of these drinks that are all natural. I also take daily vitamins and supplements to maintain a healthy body. I take an organic multivitamin every day. I take a turmeric and ginger supplement every day. I take vitamin D3 and vitamin B12 in a liquid form every day.

Movement is critical to having a healthy body. I walk thirty minutes every day. This is in addition to my daily steps. Depending on my schedule, I will walk for thirty minutes in the morning or thirty minutes in the evening. There are many forms of exercise, and this is the simplest one for me. Enjoy the outdoors and the beautiful world God has created. Just do something, and exercise your body every day.

I also spend time each week meditating. I find a quiet place in my home to use my imagination. I imagine Jesus and the Holy Spirit inside my body. They are destroying all the cancer. The image of Jesus flows through my bloodstream and removes cancer for my liver, colon, pancreas, kidneys, lungs, and other organs. Jesus cleans my body and removes all of the disease inside me. I also have the image of Jesus comforting me and healing my body. Jesus takes away my pain. I imagine myself completely healed and rejoicing with the great physician, Jesus Christ.

Another meditation technique that I use is humming my favorite church songs. I lie quietly and hum songs like "Victory in Jesus," "Amazing Grace," and "Silent Night." I hum all of those old church hymns until my memory has ended.

Listening to music is another form of meditation that I use. Summer is my favorite season, so I listen to classical music by Antonio Vivaldi called "Summer."

Cancer is a terrible disease, and those of us who are stricken with it must find ways to deal with it in our daily life. This information that I have shared with you is my approach to mentally and physically fight cancer. These processes and activities work for me. Try some of them, and see if they work in your life. You may have a different approach, but what is most important is that you never give up on life. No matter what your condition is in life, you need a strong spiritual and physical foundation. Remember that you are never alone if Jesus is Lord of your life. A support group of family and friends is also very important. Always accept help and ask for help if you need it, and stay positive.

Cancer strikes again. During my visit to the doctor to review my periodic scans, I received good news and bad news. The good news was that the CT scan showed no evidence of cancer in my lungs, liver, pancreas, stomach, bowels, spleen, and kidneys. No cancer. The bad news was that the MRI showed images of mucinous carcinoma cancer in my lower pelvic area on my prostate. The bad cancer cells have spread creating new tumors. The doctors tell me that this is very rare for mucinous carcinoma to spread to this area of the body. This recurrence happened so fast. My body is not recovered enough for another major surgery. The doctors are looking at all options. They are concerned about the bladder and the disease spreading to other organs. Minor surgery and immunotherapy are options. The doctors also found tumor DNA in my blood. There is no medical cure for this aggressive cancer inside me. I will fight to stay alive every day. God has given my doctors the knowledge and skills to treat the cancer inside me. With much prayer, I will follow their advice to find the best treatment options.

After my new cancer diagnosis, I became a little discouraged. I prayed to Jesus for guidance, and He directed me to read the book of Job in the Bible. The book of Job gave me a sense of peace and calm to my spirit. It is a wonderful message for everyone, especially those who are struggling with unforeseen problems. During all of his adversity, Job remained faithful to God. The story of Job provides us with a happy ending. Job received all of his wealth back in a greater amount than he ever had before. He had ten more children and many grandchildren and lived for another 140 years.

God has a mission in life for you and for me. Some people call it God's purpose for life. What is your mission? Pray, and listen for Jesus to tell you about your mission. I will always choose to be a good and faithful servant to God. I will not let cancer and sickness define who I am. I may be walking through the valley of the shadow of death, but I will fear no evil for God is with me. I can see the day when I am completely healed and God removes cancer from my body forever. My time on Earth is not over because God has a purpose for me.

I hope this book has helped you in some way. I am grateful to God for giving me the opportunity to tell you about my story.

MY ADVICE FOR YOU

Here is how you receive eternal life in heaven. Romans 10:9–10 (NIV) says the following: "If you confess with your mouth that Jesus is Lord and believe in your heart that God raised him from the dead, you will be saved. For with the heart, one believes and is justified, and with the mouth one confesses and is saved."

John 3:36 (ESV) says the following: "Whoever believes in the Son has eternal life; whoever does not obey the Son shall not see life, but the wrath of God remains on him."

Ephesians 2:8–9 (ESV) says the following: "For by grace, you have been saved through faith. And this is not your own doing; it is the gift of God, not a result of works, so that no one may boast."

- The kingdom of heaven is real, and you can spend eternal life with family and friends who are believers in Jesus Christ.
- Pray, and have a daily talk with God. Make Jesus Lord of your life, and engage with Him during an hour of prayer and devotion every day. Keep your faith, and never give up on life.
- Go to church.
- Tithe to the church.
- Thank God for everything.
- Find someone who loves you and make them the love of your life. Make them your partner for life.
- Your family is the most important thing on earth.
- Hug your spouse and kids every day, and tell them you love them.
- Love life, love freedom, love everyone, because God is love.
- Always tell the truth, and be kind to everyone.
- Keep a positive mental attitude. Be optimistic.
- Nothing is beyond your reach. You can be anything you want as long as you try. In every situation, by prayer and petition, with thanksgiving, present your request to God.
- Set daily goals, and make every day the best day it can be.
- Try to learn something new every day.
- If you have a dream, try everything to make it come true.

- Offer help to those who need help.
- Volunteer and give back to your community.
- Work hard at your job to earn money so you can take care of your family.
- Have a passion for work, and give your job purpose every day.
- Live close to work, and don't waste your time with a long commute.
- Save your money. Put at least 10 percent of your paycheck into savings and pay off your debt.
- Manage your money, and plan for your retirement.
- It is OK to fail at something and make mistakes, but don't get discouraged. Never stop believing in yourself because Jesus is with you every second of the day.
- Eat healthy food, and snack on fruit.
- Walk thirty minutes daily.
- Read a book or some learning material every day.
- Listen to music every day, and go to concerts.
- Travel and take vacations.
- Visit your doctor regularly.
- Get seven to eight hours of sleep each night.
- Drink water with your meals.
- Love animals, and feed the birds.
- Look at the stars.
- Again, thank God for everything!
- I will see you in heaven.